# Everyday STEAM for the Early Childhood Classroom

*Everyday STEAM for the Early Childhood Classroom* offers a rich, rewarding pathway for early childhood educators integrating the arts into STEM instruction across ages 0–8. Science, technology, engineering, and math are mainstays of early childhood curricula, but young learners can have even more engaging experiences in these subjects with the inclusion of the arts. In this comprehensive resource, early childhood educators will learn key principles for the effective teaching of STEAM in their classrooms and be guided to leverage their existing knowledge and strengths toward meaningful learning opportunities. Packed with hands-on resources, ready-to-use teaching tools, and developmentally appropriate practices, this book is ideal for in-service and pre-service educators ready to explore and experiment with STEAM.

**Margaret Merrill** has been an early childhood educator for over 35 years, with a special interest in the arts. She was an Albert Einstein Distinguished Educator Fellow and past Presidential Awardee for Excellence in Mathematics and Science Teaching.

"Reflecting on the many educational books studied throughout my 34 year career as a K–2 teacher, I have found *Everyday STEAM for the Early Childhood Classroom: Integrating the Arts into STEM Teaching* to be an outstanding, comprehensive, inspirational resource and valuable guide for educators of preschool to third grade students."

**Julie Carmichael**, *Retired K–2 Teacher, Cumberland, Maine*

"Merrill draws from passion and a wealth of experience in offering clear openings for integrating STEM and the arts. She punctuates the importance of listening to children's ideas and using the arts to expand opportunities for their brilliance to shine in many ways – a critical and much needed message for all educators."

**Brian Gravel**, *Assistant Professor of STEM Education, Tufts University*

# Everyday STEAM for the Early Childhood Classroom

## Integrating the Arts into STEM Teaching

Margaret Merrill

Routledge
Taylor & Francis Group

NEW YORK AND LONDON

First published 2024
by Routledge
605 Third Avenue, New York, NY 10158

and by Routledge
4 Park Square, Milton Park, Abingdon, Oxon, OX14 4RN

*Routledge is an imprint of the Taylor & Francis Group, an informa business*

ISBN: 9781032498195 (hbk)
ISBN: 9781032491233 (pbk)
ISBN: 9781003395614 (ebk)

DOI: 10.4324/9781003395614

Typeset in Palatino
by Newgen Publishing UK

For those who believed in my vision and inspired me to soar.

# Contents

# Preface

Many years ago, in 1994, I came across this 1990 quote by an astronomer and astrophysicist, Carl Sagan (1934–1996): "We live in a society exquisitely dependent on science and technology, in which hardly anyone knows about science and technology" in *The Portland Press Herald*. That quote resonated so strongly with me that I began to look more closely at my science curriculum and what was being taught all around me. Ultimately, it led me to take on the adventure of writing this book.

Good teaching is grounded in joy and a belief that our experiences are a journey. Even young children can benefit from a curriculum including elements of **S**cience, **T**echnology, **E**ngineering, and **M**athematics (collectively referred to as STEM disciplines). To support and improve effective science and related teaching in the early childhood years, educators need resources, guidance, and models in order to offer all their students a rich and high-quality experience with STEM disciplines. Integrating STEM content with the **A**rts (**STEAM**) can tap into educators' imaginations, experiences, and willingness to experiment with new approaches along with an expanded vision. In this book, I present a pathway for the early childhood educator to explore and experiment with STEAM on their own and with their young students.

## Why I Wrote This Book

My personal journey up to the point of writing *Everyday STEAM* is long and full of my own adventures. Teaching has been my work and delight for over 35 years. My special interests are the Arts, I am an exhibiting watercolor artist, a musician, and a former dancer who taught creative movement to young children. I also have a focus on the outdoors.

In addition to my educational training and classroom experiences, I spent a year in Washington, D.C., as an Education Fellow in the office of US Senator Joseph Liberman as part of the Albert Einstein Distinguished Educator Fellowship program. I was also honored to be recognized in 2002 as a Presidential Awardee For Excellence in Mathematics and Science Teaching. Subsequently I began my EdD program at the University of Maine.

During my program work, I studied ways to support young children and educators in the fields of STEM, with arts integrated into their STEM experiences.

As I found through my doctoral research, STEM content appeared intermittently or not at all in many early childhood classroom settings, and even in those contexts with STEM representation, the Arts were typically not included. Why this was, what the outcomes are, and whether or how it should or can be changed were questions I thought important to ask. The conclusion I came to, informed by outcomes and my teaching experiences, was that STEM content does need to change through the integration of the Arts, so all teachers of young children feel confident and excited to embark on a more comprehensive STEAM adventure. The result of my conviction is *Everyday STEAM.*

# Acknowledgments

This book emerged after many years of teaching, reflecting, and wondering if there was any merit in what I wanted to say, to share, and to inspire in others about teaching the sciences integrated with the arts. Friends and family tasked me with putting my ideas down on paper to determine if I saw worth there. I did, and so this book is the product of that journey. My thanks goes to my first readers, Julie Carmichael and Martha Naber, both experienced early childhood educators and enthusiastic reviewers. My deep gratitude goes to my son and daughter-in-law for their expert insights into all things from the natural and scientific world. Thank you to my daughter and granddaughters for their support and encouragement along the way. And a generous thank you to my Painterly companions for their patient listening and encouragement.

Appreciation and gratitude to my editors at Taylor & Francis, Olivia Powers, Alex Andrews, and Alexis O'Brien for always being there, for their patience with my frequent questions, for their guidance, and insights into my work. And always having answers to my questions. I am indebted to those at Newgen for their thoughtful and careful editing of my text.

Special thanks to all my friends and other family members for their enthusiastic response to my efforts as a writer and to my desire to offer readers a way to bring the creative arts into STEM teaching. And to my husband, Peter, who never stopped believing in me and my ability to do this work, thank you from the depth of my heart.

# Permissions

N. M. Bodecker, "When Skies Are Low and Days Are Dark," from *Snowman Sniffles and Other Verse*. Reprinted with permission from the N. M. Bodecker Literary Estate. Text copyright © 1983 by N. M. Bodecker.

Norma Farber. "Taking Turns," from *Small Wonders* by Norma Farber. Reprinted by permission of Coward-McCann. Text copyright © 1964, 1968, 1975, 1976, 1978, 1979.

Ogden Nash, "Winter Morning," from *Custard & Company* by Ogden Nash. Reprinted by permission of Curtis Brown Ltd. Text copyright © 1962.

Tony Johnston, "Wind Has Shaken Autumn Down," Reprinted by permission of the author in *Snow Towards Evening*. Text copyright © 1990 by Tony Johnston.

James Reeves, "A Pig Tale," from *The Blackbird in the Lilac*. Reprinted with permission from David Higham Associates Limited. Text copyright © 1952.

Jane Yolen, "Shepherd's Night Count," from *Dragon Night and Other Lullabies*. Originally published by Methuen Books. Reprinted by permission of Curtis Brown, Ltd. Text copyright © 1980.

# 1

# Introduction

Exploring, experimenting, testing, investigating, comparing, and learning about their world are hard work at any age, but is what young children intuitively and continuously do. We watch them engage with people, things, and events throughout each day. Early childhood-aged children, defined as birth through age 8 by the National Association for the Education of Young Children (NAEYC), are active learners in their environment. As caring teachers, guides, parents, and caregivers, we enrich their worlds in ways we believe young children can enjoy and from which they will learn. However, educators in particular may be constrained at times by the belief that young children have limited capacities to grasp many abstract or concrete concepts which are embedded in the fields of **S**cience, **T**echnology, **E**ngineering, and **M**athematics (**STEM**). Along with this perception, educators and caregivers can find or believe themselves unprepared, or so we believe, to teach STEM topics. But thankfully, and as this book will demonstrate, many STEM concepts are – or can become – inherently teachable to children of any age.

In addition to STEM concepts, children are also innately interested in the more "artistic" aspects of their lives, such as visual, musical, movement/dance, dramatics, and creative writing themes. The good news is that young children can learn many STEM concepts reinforced through the integration of these artistic elements, which broadens the realm of **STEM** to **STEAM**.

DOI: 10.4324/9781003395614-1

We, as stewards of young children's STEM experiences, can inspire, guide, and provide additionally rich and meaningful experiences through STEAM. In this book educators will learn key principles for effective teaching of STEAM in early childhood education. The ability of young children to engage in scientific practices as well as the ways educators can guide children in the learning of Science, Technology, Engineering, and Math supported and integrated with the Arts are the focus through these chapters.

It is children's innate curiosity about their world which provides the keystone for an effective STEAM curriculum. As you develop a STEAM program for your early childhood curriculum, your content will be informed and guided by the NAEYC standards for developmentally appropriate practice (DAP). In addition, recommendations from the National Science Teachers Association (NSTA), the National Council of Teachers of Mathematics (NCTM), and the Next Generation Science Standards (NGSS) provide important resources and support as you navigate these new and exciting paths of learning.

Teachers can use this book as a guide to build a STEAM program for young learners which will help them to plan a rich, engaging, inclusive, developmentally appropriate, and fun STEAM curriculum. Understanding how young children learn STEAM topics is discussed throughout the book. Along the way, we will examine the process of "scaffolding" (instructional support) and how to use it in ways that encourage children to take risks and try new things.

We all come to new situations with something called prior knowledge or how we understand our world based on earlier experiences and ways we believe events come to pass. Prior knowledge is the foundation upon which new understandings are built, so knowing what your students know guides your planning and curriculum content. Children come to many learning situations with a relatively naïve understanding, or misconception, of events and outcomes. Recognizing children's misconceptions is an important step in meaningful learning and teaching. Educators should strive to work with young learners' misconceptions instead of simply replacing them. This approach is key to building a strong foundation of knowledge for each student.

As you work to develop your STEAM program, assessing students' understanding and learning using both formative (ongoing) and summative (endpoint) formats where appropriate will guide you in your planning. Some of the foundational elements upon which you can build a rich STEAM program include the following:

◆ Find out what they know (determine prior knowledge).
◆ Identify misconceptions.
◆ Build understanding using the foundations upon which (new) knowledge can be grounded.
◆ Engage in a spectrum of STEM investigations.
◆ Implement developmentally appropriate practices for young children in real-world situations.
◆ Determine young children's developmental abilities in the STEM fields.
◆ Through inclusion of artistic elements, develop appropriate STEAM experiences for young children based on research, key principles of scientific thinking, and standards (e.g. State, NAEYC, NSTA, and NCTM standards).
◆ Integrate STEAM concepts into the instructional design for young children.

## Ways to Use This Resource and Guide in Your Classroom

*Everyday STEAM* presents the different domains of science, technology, engineering, and mathematics in ways accessible to you. You will find ways to integrate STEM content into your daily routine and to create stand-alone units of study intertwined with different areas of the arts.

Each STEM chapter in this book includes an overview of how children access relevant STEM concepts and how you, as the teacher, can capitalize on the cognitive processes children engage in while learning and re-learning content. In the different chapters, developmentally appropriate practices are highlighted, in addition to stressing the skill of *asking meaningful questions* – providing examples of what they are and how to use them effectively in your interactions with your students during exploration or experiments.

At the end of each STEM content-focused chapter you will find a grid identifying different skill sets, learning expectations, scaffolding strategies, and accessing prior knowledge skills. Additionally, at the end of each chapter you will find an Arts grid covering the different areas of the creative arts for each age level.

## How We Begin Teaching STEM

The wonder young children bring to each day and each encounter inspires and excites those who work regularly with this age group. As educators, we know that these foundational years lay down much that is important for future development in all areas of growth. Teachers of young children know and appreciate the critical importance of their work.

The creative arts, literacy, mathematics, and play have a strong presence in the early childhood classroom. These areas often make up the major focus of early childhood education programs. STEM content in many such programs is touched on but often not delved into for a host of reasons. As mentioned previously, there may be an assumption that young children are not ready or capable of learning concepts which seem advanced and abstract. However, there is some recent research (*Taking Science to School*, NRC, 2007) supporting young children's ability to understand and apply STEM concepts which seem challenging.

The remainder of this introduction will cover in more detail the three very important strategies for teaching young children STEM concepts and content: (1) accessing their prior knowledge; (2) uncovering a child's naïve understandings, also known as misconceptions; and (3) implementing ways to assess what is being understood.

## Framing Our Work with Young Children to Meet Their Needs: Developmentally Appropriate Practice (DAP)

This section is an overview of developmentally appropriate practices, which is a framework for the "best practice" approach to support young children's learning and development. The NAEYC's *"Developmentally Appropriate Practice"* (NAEYC, 2020), which is cited extensively in this section, covers this area in great detail and I recommend going to this source for more in-depth coverage.

Developmentally appropriate practice involves meeting children where they are developmentally, and providing context so they are able to reach goals which stretch them while being achievable (NAEYC, 2020). Understanding the characteristics of each age, along with best practices to promote learning and development should be used within the context of DAP for that age. We want to be able to meet each child's needs, and DAP offers relevant approaches based on research and personal experience.

Every child travels at a unique pace through each developmental stage. Knowing the child through one-on-one interactions, observation, and getting to know the family and community where the child comes from all helps to build a picture of who that child is and his/her background.

Some important areas of growth – *social-emotional, cognitive, physical, and linguistic* are all interrelated and impact each other. These relationships, and many others can be easily visualized through the use of "concept maps" which have extensively informed my understanding of the overall educational process for young children. I have included a concept map example of how developmentally appropriate practices and their domains of growth interact and influence each other (Figure 1.1).

In Figure 1.1, the map lines and arrows radiate out from the top bubble which is the main focus of this map. The four developmental areas identified in this map (smaller bubbles) are all inter-connected with lines and arrows. The connecting one-way arrows link the four sub-concepts. The bi-directional arrows show how the different sub-concepts interact with each other. For

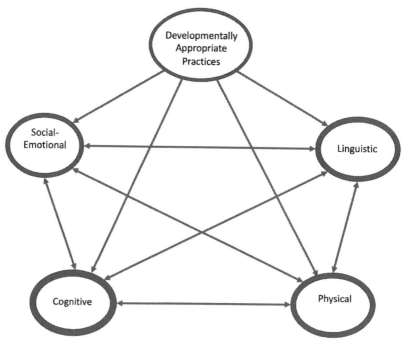

**FIGURE 1.1** Concept map: developmentally appropriate practice.

example, the social-emotional bubble is linked to the other three concepts with bi-directional arrows. This configuration indicates that a relationship exists among the different sub-concepts that are so linked. Social-emotional development is impacted by a child's linguistic, cognitive, and physical development. This configuration applies to the other three developmental concepts. All are interconnected in a young child's growth and development.

## Guidelines for Developmentally Appropriate Practice

The NAEYC has provided some guidelines for Developmentally Appropriate Practice (NAEYC, 2020).

- ◆ Creating a caring, equitable community of learners.
- ◆ Engaging in reciprocal partnerships with families and fostering community connections.
- ◆ Observing, documenting, and assessing children's development and learning.

- Teaching to enhance each child's development and learning.
- Planning and implementing an engaging curriculum to achieve meaningful goals.
- Demonstrating professionalism as an Early Childhood Educator.

## Understanding Prior Knowledge and its Place in Meaningful Learning

Prior knowledge is what each student "knows" (or understands to be valid), and brings to the classroom. This knowledge arises from direct experience, from interactions between the child and the environment. Within that environment will be other people of various ages, as well as objects, events, experiences, and sensations. Each one of these interactions and observations creates a way of thinking and knowing germane to the child as to what happened, why it happened, and its impact on the child's way of understanding. Prior knowledge is the foundation upon which new knowledge is built.

Family dynamics, social interactions, and culture bring a type of lens or way of seeing to the child's direct experience with life's events. Each category is complex and can change over time, influencing children's perceptions and ways of thinking.

Learning builds upon learning; in other words, prior knowledge – what the learner already knows is a key factor influencing additional learning. Accessing children's prior knowledge is key to meaningful learning where new concepts build upon existing ones and then are revised /or expanded.

Discovering children's own knowledge presents opportunities within the classroom. Direct questioning – asking meaningful questions – facilitates the process as does close observation of a child's conversation and actions. Close observation is giving the child all your attention, listening closely to the child's questions, looking at the child when communicating, listening to comments, chatter, and conversation between the child and others, including the teacher. It also includes self-talk the child might engage in while playing – a running commentary of sorts verbalizing thoughts, actions, interactions, and plans within a play situation.

A simple approach to gain access to students' prior knowledge is described by the *What I Know, What I Want to Learn, What I Learned* (K-W-L) chart developed by Ogle (1986). Variations on this chart have subsequently been developed by others over time but the central idea behind it remains the same: to generate and record students' prior knowledge before a study commences. During or immediately following the study, experiment, or experience, invite all students to share what they learned. This is a straightforward method of tapping into what learners believe they know about certain topics. It is a popular method many early childhood educators use in their classrooms.

This K-W-L approach opens a window into students' belief systems about a specific content topic. As an objective, descriptive process, it does not analyze, determine, or predict students' cognitive scheme of understanding. It is one approach to gaining access to students' prior knowledge.

## Defining and Understanding the Process of Asking Meaningful Questions

Meaningful questions are asked to gain insight into what a child understands while encouraging them to think and reflect in different ways. A question requiring only a "yes" or "no" response typically falls outside of the meaningful question criteria.

Meaningful questions serve multiple purposes in the classroom. They are a window into ways young children think about concepts and the ways those concepts are understood. Meaningful questions also serve to extend a child's thinking about a particular experience or activity in which they have participated. Furthermore, being a good listener as a teacher enhances the environment supporting the asking of thoughtful and meaningful questions. As a listener, make eye contact, focus your attention on the speaker, listen patiently, don't interrupt, ask follow-up questions with intent, and be responsive with body language and comments.

Using meaningful questions focuses attention on a particular aspect of something a child has just participated in or experienced through observation. Thoughtful questions aim to promote higher-order thinking, which is different from (and can complement) memorization or exact recall.

Thoughtful or meaningful questions with no right/wrong answers ask the child to engage in reflection and processing. They are questions that probe beyond recall, and should ideally not result in yes/no answers, but which instead prompt the child to reflect, connect, interpret, compare, or analyze information.

Providing engaging questions on the spot which are not yes/ no or right/wrong in nature can be challenging. It helps to anticipate and have some questions ready to ask when the situation is right. These questions can fall into several separate, but potentially overlapping categories as follows:

### Types of Questioning and Expected Response or Behavior from the Child

♦ Remember: Identify, name, count, repeat, recall.
♦ Understand: Describe, discuss, explain, summarize.
♦ Apply: Explain why, dramatize, identify with/relate to.
♦ Analyze: Recognize change, experiment, infer, compare, contrast.
♦ Evaluate: Express opinion, judge, defend/criticize.
♦ Create: Make, construct, design, author.

Example: a rose:

♦ Remember: What flower is this?
♦ Understand: Describe what you see.
♦ Apply: How do you know it is a rose?
♦ Analyze: How is this flower different from the flower next to it?
♦ Evaluate: What do you think a rose needs in order to grow?
♦ Create: How would you go about growing a rose?

This topic is developed in greater detail in the NAEYC resource: *Big Questions for Young Minds* (Strasser & Mufson Bresson, 2017).

## Misconceptions and Naïve Understandings: How We Can Work with Them to Enrich Learning

Misconceptions are ways of understanding observed and experienced events in our lives which are not in line with what is otherwise known about the events in the different science realms. Children may be expected to bring a number of preconceived and naïve understandings about how the world around them works to their school experiences. These naïve understandings can conflict with scientific teachings at times. It is not always easy for the teacher to discern student misconceptions. Children might appear to understand and accept a new explanation for an observed or experienced event while maintaining their original mental model of the event. The National Research Council (2007) suggests, in order for children to develop a conceptual framework embracing new and possible conflicting notions about the world, they need to change their way of thinking and understanding of a specific event. Where they held one set of beliefs, now they need to embrace a new way of thinking. For example, children watch cartoons and see the characters doing all sorts of antics which would result in disaster in the real world, but they perceive what is viewed as actual.

Knowledge is typically hierarchical, with new information using already established knowledge in order to build a new way of understanding. Children's conceptual knowledge builds on prior experiences, personal knowledge, and understandings, which provide foundational platforms upon which subsequent knowledge is constructed. Children acquire new information through direct experiences and classroom teachings. Children then endeavor to create coherent explanations reflecting earlier understandings of the mechanisms and classification of things. Misconceptions arise as children work to bring together earlier understandings with scientific knowledge that is not always intuitive, such as density and buoyancy. Size is the primary determining factor regarding whether an object floats or sinks in a container of water. Young children believe the bigger an object is, the more likely it is that it will sink.

Children's misconceptions can present a roadmap for guiding a student from a series of misperceptions to a more authentic understanding of a particular STEM content area (NRC, 2007). Listening closely to your students while making careful observations can reveal ways your students understand events and experiences. Following observations, you can engage the child with a series of probing questions which lead the child to reflect and question his/her own assumptions. When there is conflict between the child's way of thinking and what occurred, the conceptual issue of fitness then arises. Does the child's understanding match well with what happened? Through using guided questions, the child can be brought to look again and revise his/her way of thinking about a certain event or interaction. The concept map in Figure 1.2 illustrates these relationships.

The main idea of this concept map is the misconceptions young children bring to their experiences in the science domains. This map is arranged in a hierarchical manner with the top bubbles showing ways children gather information and how their explanations of the world around them are formed. Bubbles further down the concept map represent teaching strategies to address misconceptions informed by prior knowledge. Finally through the use of a concept map created by the learner (at the bottom of Figure 1.2), understanding can be demonstrated which then in turn informs further learning experiences.

## Moving a Young Learner Beyond His/Her Comfort Zone with Scaffolding

Giving a literal or figurative helping hand to young learners helps them move beyond physical or cognitive limitations they might

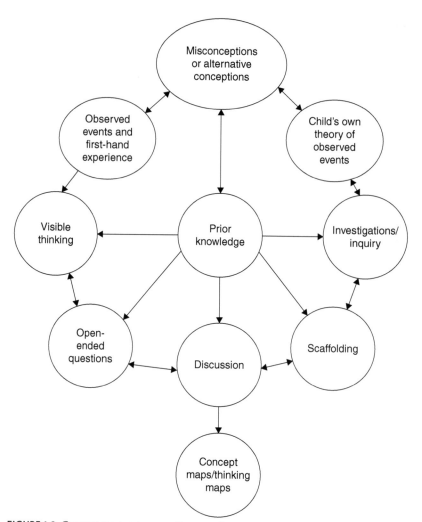

**FIGURE 1.2** Concept map: misconceptions or alternate conceptions.

bump up against. "Scaffolding" is one such helping hand. It can help bridge the gap between what a child can do on his/her own to meeting the challenge of a new task, skill, or understanding outside of the young learner's comfort zone. Scaffolding builds connections between the known and the new.

Scaffolding takes what the child knows and can do on his/her own to the next level with support from a more skilled individual (teacher, parent, or peer). Scaffolding adjusts support as the child masters the task. When the child advances to the next skill level, there is a revised application of scaffolding. The support fades as the child becomes proficient with the task and then re-emerges as the child enters a new phase of learning.

To implement scaffolding successfully it is important to know the child's developmental stage. Close observation, thoughtful questioning and knowledge of the child's social and cultural context informs you of where your student is developmentally. Taking the child from that place to a place he/she could not reach on his/her own but is ready to work toward is the goal of scaffolding. It's letting the child soar.

What does scaffolding look like? Scaffolding depends on the task and goal at hand. Praise and encouragement are a way of scaffolding, such as holding the conceptual bike handles while the child gains his/her balance; or scaffolding can be reinforcing a specific behavior through repetition. The use of direct questioning can encourage the child to think and reflect while developing awareness of a process or practice that is not intuitive. This helps your young learner move with guidance and support beyond his/her zone of competency.

Scaffolding is closely tied with constructivist learning, where the child, with support from the teacher or other adult or expert, is guided through an activity or lesson by example and thoughtful questioning.

As teachers, we integrate many approaches for guiding and supporting our students in their daily experiences. The traditional use of direct instruction can sometimes be a top-down, one-way approach for providing instruction and information. In this model, the teacher provides the information without the child having the opportunity to explore and experience on his/her own. Free exploration, which is exploration without teacher or other adult interaction, allows the learner to directly manipulate and interact with materials, coming to his/her own conclusion, which may make sense to the child, but which is not necessarily a conclusion which promotes deeper understanding. The tandem approach of free exploration combined with teacher input through careful observation of the child's actions and reactions (with thoughtful questioning) can provide the helping and guiding hand of scaffolding.

Another way to view the learning continuum is through Lev Vygotsky's Zone of Proximal Development (ZPD) (Vygotsky, 1965). Vygotsky believed children actively constructed their knowledge. An integral and key element of a child's learning experience is the social and cultural context of knowledge construction. The Zone of Proximal Development includes zones of development situated in a "lower limit" where the child is able to problem-solve on his/her own. These zones extend to an "upper limit" where the child, with support and help from a more skilled individual such as the teacher, parent, or peer, is able to accomplish the task at hand. The use of the helping hand and careful support for each young learner can move the student from "stuck" to "soaring."

## Knowing What Our Students Are Learning: Informal Assessment

As educators, we spend a lot of time observing our young learners play and interact with each other and with their early childhood environment. We learn much from our time spent watching each child, such as whether the child engages in solo play, parallel play (side-by-side play without interacting with the other child or children), or collaborative play. This is the first layer of assessment, also known as informal assessment. Using the meaningful question guide, a teacher can get a strong sense of what the child understands and of his/her mental model. As previously stated, prior knowledge is the foundation upon which new knowledge is built. Knowing what the child understands prior to the lesson or activity compared with what the child understands following the lesson or activity informs the teacher about the child's construction of knowledge.

Earlier in this Introduction I demonstrated a method of understanding a concept through creating a concept map. This is an alternative method of informal assessment known as a visual representation strategy. Concept maps allow the child to show what he/she knows through the arrangement and organization of the concepts or boxes within the map. Young children are able to create such maps with adequate support from adults. Pictures can be used in addition to text to show how the child understands a concept or idea.

## Include Those Who Know Your Student Best: Family Outreach and Inclusion

I have found when families are made welcome in the classroom, trust blossoms on both sides. When families feel welcomed, they become partners in their child's journey of growth and learning. As partners, parents and primary caregivers become a valuable resource in many ways. Creating an environment where parents or primary caregivers become partners with the teachers promotes a two-way partnership with the people who matter most to the individual child and his/her progress and success.

Families and primary caregivers can provide a wealth of information and support for the early childhood classroom their child attends. They are the experts who know the child best. They provide cultural context in which the child is growing up. When included openly into the early childhood program, families can provide classroom support while also offering knowledgeable or expert insights into curriculum areas. Families can provide resources supporting classroom activities, investigations, and field trips.

Making families welcome in the classroom by keeping doors and communication open precludes many problems that arise when families feel unwelcome in the classroom or are unfamiliar with the program, teachers, curriculum, and expectations in the classroom. Including those who know your learner best is a win-win situation for everyone.

## How Children Learn Best and Brain Development in Early Childhood

In *A New Path to Education Reform: Playful Learning Promotes 21st-Century Skills in Schools and Beyond*, Kathy Hirsh-Pasek and Helen Hadani (2020) identified six skill sets (6 Cs) children should experience throughout their early learning years in order to meet the challenges of a changing world, or as the Brookings Institution (Hirsh-Pasek & Hadini, 2022) has labeled it, "skills for a changing world." According to the authors, "collaboration, or social relationships are the foundation for an interconnected suite of skills."

The 6 Cs are:

1. Collaboration
2. Communication
3. Content
4. Critical thinking
5. Creative innovation
6. Confidence.

## How the Foundation for Learning Success Is Built in Early Childhood: The Science of Brain Development in Early Childhood

As educators and childcare providers, we know intuitively what very young children require to thrive: a caring community, establishing reciprocal relationships with families and communities, and, most importantly, establishing reciprocal caring and attentive relationships between the child and the adults in the child's life.

The Center on the Developing Child at Harvard University (2007) lists six additional key components for healthy brain development in very young children. The pivotal interaction between adult and child is the "serve and return" exchange between child and parent, caregiver, or others within the child's immediate community. "Serve and return" is when the child and adult interact with positive and caring responses – the adult smiles and laughs, the child responds, the adult responds back with additional positive attention. All this builds trust within a caring relationship between the young child and the attentive adult.

Those six foundational ingredients for healthy brain development in the young child are:

1. Child development is a foundation for community development and economic development, as capable children

become the foundation of a prosperous and sustainable society.

2. Brains are built over time.

3. The interactive influences of genes and experience literally shape the architecture of the developing brain, and the active ingredient is the "serve and return" nature of children's engagement in relationships with their parents and other caregivers in their family or community.

4. Both brain architecture and developing abilities are built "from the bottom up," with simple circuits and skills providing the scaffolding for more advanced circuits and skills over time.

5. Toxic stress in early childhood is associated with persistent effects on the nervous system and stress hormone systems that can damage developing brain architecture and lead to lifelong problems in learning, behavior, and both physical and mental health.

6. Creating the right conditions for early childhood development is likely to be more effective and less costly than addressing problems at a later age.

Studies by the Center on the Developing Child make clear the critical importance of building a strong and supportive foundation for early childhood growth, not only through school engagement, but through community involvement. The tennis-like "serve and return" behavior noted above is foundational for the healthy development of children. It is the caring and reciprocal interaction between a caregiver of importance and the child which then builds trust and allows the child to know and have trust in those around him. This social interaction also helps to build the foundation for the interconnected collection of the 6Cs. As Dr. Shonkoff states, "genes and experience shape the architecture of the developing brain" (Center on the Developing Child at Harvard University, 2007), noting that the most important ingredient is the give and take or active social, emotional, and physical interaction between caregiver and child. Awareness of how genes and experience impact brain development helps us as teachers and helps all others who care for and work with young children to create and deliver a curriculum which fosters these elements.

## A Look at Lesson Plans and Activities

Throughout this book you will find suggested activities to accompany many of the STEAM areas. Activities are simple one-on-one or small group exercises that do not require a lot of pre-planning or organization. They are opportunities to engage with your learner in a relaxed and playful atmosphere. They are also suggestions to help your imagination to take over and allow you to try new things and explore your own ideas. Activities also are times when you can closely observe, ask meaningful questions, and scaffold learning.

Lesson plans have a format which you are free to adapt as needed. They do require more planning and organization and will generally involve the whole class, at least initially while the lesson is introduced. Children then can work in small groups or alone as the lesson allows.

The format of the lesson plans include age range, objective, and learning target. Guiding practices will be listed such as "activating prior knowledge," and "open-ended questions." Suggested steps to accomplish the lesson are laid out for you. An informal assessment is suggested for use at the conclusion of the lesson. Ask these two key questions: *Were all the children engaged? Were all the children able to participate?* These lessons are only suggestions and a way to help you get started. Adapt and adjust as you see fit for your students and your curriculum needs. You are the one on this journey of discovery along with your young explorers. Enjoy!

## A Concluding Introductory Thought: Let's Look at Bias in the Classroom

What is bias? In NAEYC's *Anti-Bias Education for Young Children and Ourselves*, Louise Derman-Sparks and Julie Olsen Edwards

(2012) nicely define bias: an attitude, belief, or feeling that results in and helps to justify unfair treatment of a person because of his or her identity. Bias is also a broader attitude, belief, or feeling about events, objects, or occurrences we encounter in our day-to-day lives.

An encounter between an adult and a preschooler demonstrated how a seemingly simple personal attitude was displayed conveying bias. The adult and preschool-aged girl were examining a diorama filled with different animals. They spent some time identifying the animals found in the scene until they came to the snake. The adult identified the animal using a voice conveying dislike for the animal. No doubt the adult did not like snakes, but to convey this attitude, this bias, to the young girl sent a message: snakes have something about them which is not desirable. To the adult, it was a gut reaction to circumstances, however, the implications can run deep. Our days are filled with reactions just like this one, unpremeditated, but conveying bias about a belief regarding others, events, circumstances, or objects.

To become aware of bias, we need to be willing to reflect and consider our belief systems. We view our world through a lens influenced, over the course of our lives, by our environment and our experiences. Our biases can be small or subtle, or not so small or subtle, but developing an awareness of having and reacting to them can help us achieve a better understanding of our own actions, attitudes, and feelings as well as how they may impact others under our tutelage.

While completing research for my doctorate, a section on bias was to be included in my writing. I believed I didn't have biases, but I metaphorically began using a microscope to look closely at my perceptions, and found I did have biases. We bring assumptions to most circumstances and encounters with others and events. These assumptions open the door for bias to influence what we see and think we understand.

A tone of voice, body language, and choice of words all convey a message. What are your expectations regarding gender, culture, racial identity, economic class, family structure, different abilities, and holidays? Examine your classroom organization, choice of books, color assumptions, play preferences, opportunities which are provided for different groups of children. Do you think your tone is different when addressing boys or girls? What are your expectations when children are in the dramatic play area, dress-up area, or building area? Look closely and carefully, is there bias in spite of best intentions?

A thoughtful STEAM curriculum is an opportunity to address bias which comes with STEM topics and the arts. Our culture and society have historically expected males to dominate in many of the sciences, technology, engineering, and math domains. Along with gender expectations in sports and other disciplines, these expectations have slowly evolved for STEM-related applications but can persist in subtle ways. All children enjoy the arts: however, we often look to the girls for greater creativity and "artistic" success in the early years. In certain circumstances girls can sit for longer periods and their small motor skills often develop before their male counterparts. This does not mean all boys will not have these abilities at the same developmental age as the girls; it is a generalization. Yet, historically, our culture has recognized adult male artists over adult female artists. This is also evident in the world of STEM research and practice.

Once again, for in-depth explorations into all the many different biases we consciously or unconsciously may bring with us and encounter, I recommend NAEYC's comprehensive and worthwhile publication *Anti-Bias Education for Young Children and Ourselves*, by Louise Derman-Sparks and Julie Olsen Edwards (2012). This book examines not only gender bias, but culture, racial identity, economic class and fairness, family structures, different abilities, and holidays.

As you read the individual chapters in the remainder of this book, please remember that you are also on an unending journey of discovery along with your young explorers … so I hope you too enjoy the ride.

# 2

# The Joy of Creative Arts

## Introduction

To dance, to sing, to create with freedom releases the soul. The creative arts encompass creative expression from all regions of our brain and body. The arts are an integral part of our lives, our experiences and pleasures, and our expressions. Children thrive on experiencing the creative arts. It is a chance for them to show their thoughts, feelings, and interests through all the different avenues creative arts collectively afford.

The creative arts include theater/drama/puppetry, music, dance/movement, visual arts, creative writing, and photography/filming. Young children take naturally to all of these forms of expressions, which are useful for extending, enhancing, and enriching the STEM topics covered in this book.

Integrating the creative arts with STEM is a logical extension of the work you as teachers are already doing. Integrating the arts into STEM areas takes planning for time, space, materials, and execution, but is exciting and rewarding for all.

A lesson plan is found at the end of this chapter, and illustrates a blended example of the following individual areas covered in this chapter.

DOI: 10.4324/9781003395614-2

## Theater/Drama/Puppetry

Young children are natural play actors. They love to dress up and invent a storyline of their own imagining or of some well-known story they have heard over and over. Dramatic display opens a door for fun and imaginative STEM integration. Theater for young children can be many different things; it can be a real on-stage experience re-enacting a story, or can be just an expressive experience where children follow their own impulses and reactions. Children can improvise a response to a specific prompt or use puppets to respond to the prompt. Theater is a safe place for children to express themselves creatively without judgment. Using hand-held puppets adds another element to this domain. Puppets can be made by children and used by children, used by adults, or both. Puppets are fascinating to children. Youngsters are highly responsive to them, in spite of knowing they are controlled by the person holding the puppet's strings. Using hand-held puppets is easier than holding the puppet. A STEM theme can direct choices of play topics. Table 2.1 illustrates some examples of these options and relationships.

## Music

Music touches many parts of our lives. It heals, comforts, energizes, and has a way of reaching deep down into our hearts and souls to move us. Music as an extension of STEM activities does not need to be complicated or involved. Simply clapping a rhythm or accompanying a poem or story with responses, either vocal or percussive, can bring music into the lesson or activity. Music includes but is not limited to the domains of: (1) Percussion – creating sound with the striking of one object with another; (2) Rhythm – a strong regular repeated pattern of sound or movement; (3) Tonality, which reflects on the overall quality of a vocal or musical sound; and (4) Dynamics, such as slow-fast,

**TABLE 2.1** Creative arts with STEM: theater/drama/puppetry

| Theater topic | Example | STEM tie-in | Activity |
|---|---|---|---|
| Children's theater: simple script children follow – scripted form of activity | Choose a STEM theme-based story or poem to dramatize with some scripting for children to speak or act | Story: Three Little Pigs<br><br>Engineering, patterns, size, prediction, physics (force and motion – houses falling down in response to a force) revise story to have the houses fall down due to storms or wind or other natural occurrences | Simple script of Three Little Pigs<br><br>Revise, rewrite, or change some parts of the story to tie in with your theme – such as the little pigs exploring the engineering principles (see Chapter 5)<br><br>Use meaningful questions to guide children into the story |
| Improvisation: respond to a prompt | Provide a prompt: picture/item/word which can be a short sentence or phrase and have children freely react to the prompt | Prompt examples:<br><br>Picture: animal (recognizable to children)<br>Item: a marble (something from either the classroom or home)<br>Word: under | This activity is good for older children – Kindergarten through third grade. They act out their prompt either alone or collaborate together creating a simple skit. |
| Puppets | Puppets can tell a story by acting it out. They can be controlled by adults or children. Puppets can run the gamut of expression and action. Children can ad lib a story a puppet is telling by adding information and building the story. Children can act out a simple story line or plot with puppets. Puppets can be hand-held, cut-outs, small, or large. They can be used as silhouettes to tell a story. | Poem: "Shepherd's Night Count" by Jane Yolen (see Chapter 6)<br>One ewe,<br>One ram,<br>Two sheep,<br>One flock,<br>Four gates,<br>One lock,<br>Five folds,<br>One light,<br>Good dog,<br>Good night. | Puppet play with a focus on counting. |

(Continued)

**TABLE 2.1** (*Continued*)

| STEM | Examples |
|------|----------|
| Science | Life cycles, habitats, seasons, chemical reactions, motion and stability, earth science systems, rocks, water (oceans, streams, lakes, ponds, rivers, etc.), solar system |
| Technology | Robots<br>Recording video or sound<br>Digital media games<br>Whiteboard or other digital technology to capture information |
| Engineering | Identify a problem, design a solution, build, test, assess, re-design, test<br>Cause and effect<br>Creating shapes |
| Math | Numbers and number sense, counting, number operations<br>Patterns<br>Measurement<br>Shape<br>Spatial relationships<br>Geometry |

loud-soft, high-low, short-long, and so on. Table 2.2 contains examples of these musical domains.

## Singing

Young children sing without inhibition or restraint while adults are often confined by their judgment of their own voice and pitch. Singing releases the inner voice quite literally and gives wing to joy. A piece of advice for the inhibited adult singer – *sing-out* with bravado, strength, and volume regardless of how you believe you sound. It is the joy you may show which makes singing a delight for your listeners and will inspire your young singers to join in.

Singing comes in many forms – chants which are phrases repeated in more of a sing-song than full song. Singing is typically repetitive, with phrases that can come around again and again, teaching pattern and predictability. There are fun action songs where the lyrics are acted out in movement which also can be repetitive. Lots of fun can be had with the call and response form of singing. One person calls out a phrase or sings out a phrase and all others respond. The response can be an echo of the call or it can truly be a response. Play, take risks, enjoy singing.

Music can recreate sounds found in nature (wind, rain, ocean, storms, etc.) Patterns in music and singing can reinforce numbers, prediction, similarities, and differences. Singing also gives children experience with repetition, patterns, and prediction, while lyrics can be focused on different STEM content. STEM content integrates easily with both music and singing. See Table 2.3 for suggested activities to do with different forms of singing.

## Movement/Dance

Children move physically throughout their day in many ways which take them to many different places. Movement is expression, a way to demonstrate emotion, or simply a way to get from one

TABLE 2.2 Creative arts with STEM: music

| Music topic | Example | STEM tie-in | Activity |
|---|---|---|---|
| Percussion | Creating a sound by hitting two objects together or shaking an object<br><br>Drums, sticks, spoons, musical instruments: drums, cymbals, gongs, bells, rattles, xylophones | Sound, patterns, determining and choosing appropriate items for use, identifying and classifying types of sounds from different objects, identifying objects which create loud or soft percussive sounds<br><br>Classify, organize, count, and sets | Whole class, small group, or classroom stations explore the themes of percussion. Record on chart paper or on a whiteboard the information for children to see and to share<br><br>Provide a variety of items for children to choose from to explore and experiment with<br><br>Ask meaningful questions to encourage reflective thinking. |
| Rhythm | A strong, regular, repeated pattern of sound or movement | All STEM: Prediction and pattern recognition<br><br>Math: Creating and copying pattern, extending pattern<br><br>Identifying qualities of the rhythm/pattern<br><br>Choosing ways to make a rhythm – clap, pat hands on legs or other item, stomp or tap with shoes or feet, snap fingers, nod the head or move the whole body in response to a rhythm (space orientation–geometry)<br><br>Technology: Record rhythm pattern, video movement | Whole class, small group, or classroom station for children to be introduced to the notion of rhythm, explore the nature of rhythm through listening, echoing, copying, or creating. Explore objects and determine those good for use as a rhythm instrument. |
| Clapping | The best sort of music making instrument – clapping with the hands | Math: patterns, fast, slow, loud, soft, counting, sorting (types of claps – quick, soft, slow, loud), spatial orientation – copying someone, mirroring someone, clap in different spaces (near the body, above the head, clap with your partner)<br><br>Technology: film, record, share<br><br>Science: recreate sounds from nature with types of clapping: animal sounds, water sounds, crashing sounds | Whole class, small groups, classroom stations – copy a clapping pattern written up on a whiteboard, chart paper, strip of construction paper (different symbols for different types of claps), creating a clapping pattern and record it on paper or with recording device |

| | | | |
|---|---|---|---|
| Tone | Duration<br>Pitch – degree of highness or lowness of a tone<br>Timbre (quality) | Identifying different tones – not something to spend a lot of time on, but useful for clarification and insight into music components when singing for a performance | Experiment with tones using the voice or other objects which might be or might not be appropriate for exploring tones. Children will decide on objects which work best for them through exploration and experimentation for sensing and exploring tone. |
| Dynamic | Volume of a sound (relative)<br>Loud, soft<br>Fast, slow<br>Ascending, descending<br>Short, long<br>Gradual, abrupt<br>Harsh, soft<br>Single, group<br>Use of silence | Dynamics of a sound once again not something to spend a lot of time on but useful for clarification and insights into music definitions when singing or performing<br>Identification of loud and soft<br>Identifying objects appropriate (or not) for creating loud or soft sounds including the voice | Experiment with the dynamics of a song or piece of music to differentiate loud from soft, fast from slow |

| *STEM* | *Examples* |
|---|---|
| Science | Life cycles, habitats, seasons, chemical reactions, motion and stability, earth's systems, rocks, water (oceans, streams, lakes, ponds, rivers, etc.), solar system |
| Technology | Robots<br>Recording video or sound<br>Digital media games<br>Whiteboard or other digital technology to capture information |
| Engineering | Identify a problem, design a solution, build, test, assess, re-design, test<br>Cause and effect<br>Creating shapes |
| Math | Numbers and number sense, counting number operations, patterns, measurement, shape, spatial relationships, geometry |

**TABLE 2.3** Creative arts with STEM: singing

| Singing topic | Example | STEM tie-in | Activity |
|---|---|---|---|
| Chants | Chanting is similar to talking with a rhythm and rhyming words and phrases. Chants can also instruct with an play action or game with a goal or end product/result. They are simple and repetitive. Can also be used to give directions to children in a sing-song/chant form. | Chants are repetitious, tell a story, are simple forms of singing or sharing a direction or other type of information. Chants can have hand or other simple movement actions accompanying them. Math and other STEM topics are a natural tie-in with patterns and predictions. A chant can be made up on the spot to direct attention to an activity, an event, or get children's attention. They do have rhyming qualities to them. | Take a nursery rhyme or short repetitious story and put it into a chant form. Teach it to the children then have them do it with you or echo you. This includes movement, careful listening, copying, and maybe if it is appropriate, improvise movements or build on the chant. The chant focus can be about any STEM topic which is of interest to your students. Get your students up and moving around with chants – this helps with spatial orientation, movement through space which is important for geometry. |
| Repetition | There is a lot of repetition in singing. The chorus in songs is repetition, the song itself has a repetitious element to it – verse/chorus/verse/chorus, and so on. | There are many repetitious songs available for teaching to young children. Some of the songs build verse upon verse with the chorus in between. These singing experiences teach prediction and pattern. Along with the text of the song which can relate to most STEM topics. | The suggested activities in the box above can be used for experiencing repetition in singing |
| Action/play songs | These are songs with action often building over the duration of the song into a singing play. They are lots of fun for everyone. | Action/play songs work well with engineering activities. Building, creating, organizing. Action/play songs require children to follow directions, cooperate with the lead singer and classmates, and move. Movement through space and time is an activity important for spatial awareness and geometry skills. | "Mississippi Boatman's Song" *Oh the boatman dance, the boatman sing, the boatman do most everything.* Act, change what the boatman can do, change the boatman to the child, the … (tie in with a STEM topic – nature – turtle) "The turtle can do most everything" |

| Call and response | One person speaks, chants, calls, or sings a line or phrase and the class repeats it or responds to it | Calls can be anything, a song the children are learning, a question and response format – asking good questions<br><br>Giving directions<br><br>Inviting participation and engagement<br><br>STEM topics are all appropriate for this form of singing. | A call and response format is a pattern with a predictable shape and form. It can be changed at any time by either the caller or the responders.<br><br>*Call: Hello*<br><br>*Response: Hello*<br>*How are you?*<br><br>*How are you?* (Or it can be changed to an answer) – *I am fine.*<br><br>The call and response can direct children's actions which tie in with classroom STEM activities – counting, moving around in specific ways, creating a whole class project. |

| *STEM* | *Examples* |
| --- | --- |
| Science | Life cycles, habitats, seasons, chemical reactions, motion and stability, earth's systems, rocks, water (oceans, streams, lakes, ponds, rivers, etc.), solar system |
| Technology | Robots<br>Recording video or sound<br>Digital media games<br>Whiteboard or other digital technology to capture information |
| Engineering | Identify a problem, design a solution, build, test, assess, re-design, test<br>Cause and effect<br>Creating shapes |
| Math | Numbers and number sense, counting number operations, patterns, measurement, shape, spatial relationships, geometry |

Note: See Resources chapter for children's song books.

point to another. Sometimes the movements evolve into a dance which is precise and choreographed. Movement is the foundation for dance and all other forms of bodily action. Dance, like all other forms of artistic expression, opens a door within – allowing each of us to respond to some external or internal impulse which inspires and moves us. Dance and movement take us through time and space, giving free expression to different forms of display and bodily combinations of shapes and gestures.

Providing time for young children to play with movement and dance elements gives them a foundational sense and understanding of ways the body can move and how they can control it. The vocabulary of movement enhances young learners' sense of spatial awareness as their body moves through space.

Movement and dance are natural enhancers of many STEM topics. Different topics can be experienced, explained, and internalized through the different extensions and opportunities offered through movement and dance. See Table 2.4 for movement and creative dance activities.

## Visual Arts

This area of the creative arts can provide familiar and comfortable mechanisms interfacing with STEM topics to incorporate into our lessons. There are many aspects of the visual arts which are a natural for all children to explore and enjoy. Children will have preferences within the different visual arts. Help each child find his or her comfort area. This will give you insights into ways to extend and scaffold new experiences and opportunities for each child to express their ideas through the visual arts. See Table 2.5 for visual arts activities.

## Creative Writing

Creative writing is accessible to all children. Young learners have ideas to share. Being able to record thoughts on paper or through audio recordings validates the child's work. Children can dictate

**TABLE 2.4** Creative arts with STEM: movement

| Movement | Example | STEM tie-in | Activity |
|---|---|---|---|
| *Spatial Sense*<br>Close<br>Far<br>Under<br>Around<br>Over<br>On top of<br>Next to | Where a person is located in relation to something or someone else | Geometry, spatial awareness<br>Mapping<br>Engineering<br>Planning | Create an obstacle course for children to navigate using specific position vocabulary – close, far, under, around, over, on top of, next to, for example |
| Time | Slow, fast, moderately fast or moder ately slow | Math: measurement<br>Duration<br>Cycles, seasons | Movement directions – move fast, slow, faster than, slower than |
| *Dynamics of movement*<br>Relaxed<br>Delicate<br>Soft<br>Light<br>Fleeting<br>Strong<br>Tense<br>Powerful<br>Heavy<br>Energetic | How one moves over time and through space. | Geometry, spatial awareness, shape, orientation in space | Children are movers, give them language to define their own style of being and moving. This can translate to other circumstances and examples. |

*(Continued)*

**TABLE 2.4** (*Continued*)

| Movement | Example | STEM tie-in | Activity |
| --- | --- | --- | --- |
| *Types of movement*<br>Walking<br>Running<br><br>Bouncing<br>Skipping<br>Jumping<br>Turning<br>*Movement in place*<br>Bending and straightening<br>Rotating inwards and twisting<br>Swaying with transfer of weight<br>Movement combinations | How we move in place or through space | Spatial awareness, mirroring, copying, body awareness which extends to shape and geometry | Combine dynamics of movement, time, spatial sense with types of movement in place or through space to provide children with fun opportunities to be expressive, to use the space, and to respond to specific directions. Example:<br><br>"Walk fast from this corner to another corner in a straight line." "Move around the ball slowly close to the ground." Drums, tambourines, or any sort of percussion/rhythm instrument are a good accompaniment and help with the types of movement and following directions. "When I stop beating the drum, you stop in a long (or any other type of shape) shape." |
| *Dance*<br>Simple folk dances<br>Repetitive forms making a simple choreographed dance | Folk, choreographed, expressive, modern, jazz | Timing, shape, pattern, repetition, sequencing | Dance is a wonderful expression of so much – joy, music, moving with others, and personal expression. There is much to choose from – traditional forms, forms created just for your students, students, creating dance movements for them to share. |

A way to express an idea, emotion, event, or thought through repeated patterns of movement

Ballet
Modern dance
Jazz

| STEM | Examples |
| --- | --- |
| Science | Life cycles, habitats, seasons, chemical reactions, motion and stability, earth's systems, rocks, water (oceans, streams, lakes, ponds, rivers, etc.), solar system |
| Technology | Robots<br>Recording video or sound<br>Digital media games<br>Whiteboard or other digital technology to capture information |
| Engineering | Identify a problem, design a solution, build, test, assess, re-design, test<br>Cause and effect<br>Creating shapes |
| Math | Numbers and number sense, counting number operations, patterns, measurement, shape, spatial relationships, geometry |

Note: See Resources chapter for dance/movement books.

**TABLE 2.5** Creative arts with STEM: visual arts

| Visual arts | Example | STEM tie-in | Activity |
|---|---|---|---|
| Sculpture | Paper, natural materials, soft and hard materials, small or large items | Engineering<br>Math<br>Prediction<br>Patterns | Recreate an object from nature in a sculpture<br>Sculpt a shape from a math lesson on geometry and shapes |
| Pottery | Clay, plasticine | Engineering<br>Math<br>Science: nature, earth systems<br>Cause and effect<br>Physics<br>Technology: record work | Design and build a shape or a structure as it ties in with math or engineering skills<br>Cause and effect, e.g. what will happen if …? |
| Painting | Finger, brush, straw blowing, marble rolling, eye dropper, sponge painting | Chemistry: mixing different color solutions<br>Exploring mixing different primary colors<br>Cause and effect<br>Prediction<br>Exploration and experimentation | Experiment with different ways of applying paint to different surfaces (paper, wood, rocks, clay, cloth) |
| Collage | Use recycled items | Environmental education: use recycled items | Whole class, small group, individual collage project possibilities:<br>Depict a scene from a STEM-related story, poem, song, play<br>Create a collage showing the different recycled items and how they are able to be reused |

| | | Examples | |
|---|---|---|---|
| Textiles | Yarn, string, cotton cloth, wool, different fabric materials | Science – nature, environmental education<br>Chemistry: how different textiles react to cutting, pasting, sewing, gluing<br>Math: measurement<br>Prediction, patterns | Design a creature or plant with different textiles<br>Dictate a story about where it lives and why it likes living there |

*STEM*     *Examples*

| | |
|---|---|
| Science | Life cycles, habitats, seasons, chemical reactions, motion and stability, earth's systems, rocks, water (oceans, streams, lakes, ponds, rivers, etc.), solar system |
| Technology | Robots<br>Recording video or sound<br>Digital media games<br>Whiteboard or other digital technology to capture information |
| Engineering | Identify a problem, design a solution, build, test, assess, re-design, test<br>Cause and effect<br>Creating shapes |
| Math | Numbers and number sense, counting number operations, patterns, measurement, shape, spatial relationships, geometry |

to an adult who writes down their impressions or the child can make use of images from the internet, magazines, or from digital photos taken of an activity or project. These all can be used as part of their creative writing work.

Sharing many different examples of creative writing will foster young children's ability to imagine ways they want to show and share their ideas. Regular readings of different styles of poetry and stories provides models from which young children learn. Engage your young learners with a range of poetry styles and themes. Throughout this book, I include poems which tie into the particular theme of a chapter. The poems are playful, fanciful, silly, and serious. They engage the imagination with language, imagery, and repetition.

Encourage young writers to try different styles as they work on different forms of creative writing. For young children to capture their experiences and impressions of the STEM topics, creative writing provides an outlet favored by many learners. See Table 2.6 for activities for creative writing.

## Photography/Filming

Cell phones are part of our world's daily culture now and all mobile phones have the capacity to take photos and videos. Taking advantage of this technology to enrich STEM experiences is a lot of fun. Children enjoy seeing themselves in photos or on video doing funny, silly, dramatic things. Photos or videos provide wonderful opportunities for conversations about the activities in the photo or video, meaningful questions can be asked and discussions can ensue. They can provide the springboard for the next phase of an investigation or experiment – to see what happens next.

Children can add text or voice recordings to explain the images. Photography and filming offer young children a different form of expression, one which they are most likely familiar with from home and family usage. The use of photography and filming as a way of extending learning of STEM topics will be novel and exciting to young learners. See Table 2.7 for filming and photography activities.

**TABLE 2.6** Creative arts with STEM: creative writing

| Creative writing | Example | STEM tie-in | Activity |
|---|---|---|---|
| Poetry | Silly, humorous<br><br>Nature theme<br><br>Repetitive format<br><br>Meaning, sound, rhythm<br><br>Nursery rhymes | All STEM topics are appropriate for a poetry session | Prompt: children react to a poem with a poem/response of their own in pictures, words, or painting.<br><br>Asking meaningful questions helps focus and inform writers. The poem activity can be whole class or small group, or individual.<br><br>Children can make a recording if easier than writing for them. |
| Journals | Nature, data, picture journal, personal journal | Journals are appropriate for all STEM domains.<br><br>Children can record, write, draw, predict<br><br>Math: use for numeracy activities<br><br>Science: nature journal<br><br>Engineering: plan a design<br><br>Technology: a journal can be a series of recordings a child makes about a chosen topic or activity | Following a nature walk, children write in their journals. If writing is not appropriate, they can draw what they saw or dictate to someone who can write.<br><br>Take photos while out exploring the natural environment for children to use as prompts or to have for reference or to use in their own journals.<br><br>Children are encouraged to look carefully when out walking so they can write or draw in their journals when returning to the classroom. |

*(Continued)*

**TABLE 2.6** (*Continued*)

| Creative writing | Example | STEM tie-in | Activity |
|---|---|---|---|
| Story | Fiction, non-fiction, relating a sequence of events to create a story | All STEM domains are appropriate for story writing | Story writing is good for Kindergarten on up. |
| | | | Asking meaningful questions will help focus ideas for your young writers and help them reflect on what they want to write about. |
| | | | This can be a whole class activity, small group, or individual. |
| | | | Environmental education for a story topic. A day outside in the woods. |
| Expressive writing | This form of writing allows and encourages young writers or any age child with ideas to embrace them and record them either on paper or with the use of a recording device | Children can be encouraged to reflect on a STEM-related activity with expressive writing | Expressive writing is good for Kindergarten age and older. This does not mean younger children cannot explore and experiment with expressive writing, they can be introduced to it and given time and space to explore this sort of writing with support. |
| | | | Asking meaningful questions will focus ideas for your young writers and help them reflect on what they want to write about. |
| | | | This can be a whole class activity, small group, or individual. |

| STEM | Examples |
|------|----------|
| Science | Life cycles, habitats, seasons, chemical reactions, motion and stability, earth's systems, rocks, water (oceans, streams, lakes, ponds, rivers, etc.), solar system |
| Technology | Robots<br>Recording video or sound<br>Digital media games<br>Whiteboard or other digital technology to capture information |
| Engineering | Identify a problem, design a solution, build, test, assess, re-design, test<br>Cause and effect<br>Creating shapes |
| Math | Numbers and number sense, counting number operations, patterns, measurement, shape, spatial relationships, geometry |

**TABLE 2.7** Creative arts with STEM: photography/filming

| Filming/ photography | Example | STEM tie-in | Activity |
|---|---|---|---|
| Filming | Filming as part of a documentation Filming as part of a display – video can be embedded in many different platforms: website, email, text, in a digital frame which runs continuously on a loop with images uploaded. | All STEM domains are appropriate for film opportunities | An adult can film an activity, a project, an experiment Children can also take on a filming role – Kindergarten on up. This does not mean younger children should not have an opportunity to explore and experiment with support if they are interested. They should have an opportunity to experience filming if it is appropriate. |
| Photography | Photos as part of a documentation Photos as part of a display Nature photos for display / journals/projects | All STEM domains are appropriate for photo opportunities | Record either with video or photos on nature walks, capture images of experiments such as cooking projects in photos. Share on different media platforms for family participation and for class sharing. |

| STEM | Examples |
|---|---|
| Science | Life cycles, habitats, seasons, chemical reactions, motion and stability, earth's systems, rocks, water (oceans, streams, lakes, ponds, rivers, etc.), solar system |
| Technology | Robots Recording video or sound Digital media games Whiteboard or other digital technology to capture information |
| Engineering | Identify a problem, design a solution, build, test, assess, re-design, test Cause and effect Creating shapes |
| Math | Numbers and number sense, counting number operations, patterns, measurement, shape, spatial relationships, geometry |

Integrating the creative arts into STEM content releases the inner voice of your young students. It offers a platform for inquiry, investigation, exploration, and experimentation in addition to the joyful expression of the creative arts.

## The Creative Arts and STEM Lesson Plan

### Bringing It All Together

The lesson plan is appropriate at any point during your STEM journey. Substitute any STEM topic into the lesson plan and explore, experiment, and enjoy the integration of the creative arts into that topic.

This lesson plan can be taught over a period of days using the same format. Break the activities up as appropriate for your students. By asking meaningful questions before beginning a new segment of this lesson, you will be able to determine what children have understood and how they are thinking about the creative arts and STEM.

The creative arts and STEM lesson can be modified or expanded as it works for you, your time, and space, and your students. Change or adjust as needed for your own purposes. This is in part a template to be personalized. Have fun!

- ◆ Age range: 3/4–8 years old, Preschool/Early Elementary.
- ◆ Instructional objective: Introduce the integration of the creative arts with STEM teaching.
- ◆ Learning target: Introduce STEAM to young children and weave in STEM with the different creative arts forms. The focus is on the different ways we can express ourselves as we go through our day. Each day we encounter STEM topics but at this time, the emphasis is on the arts.
  - ◆ Example: the creative arts helps us share discoveries, things we care about, new ideas, and exciting insights experienced along the way as we explore science, technology, engineering, and math. The creative arts gives us opportunities to express our feelings,

share insights, and commitment to our life journey of learning.

◆ Activate prior knowledge: Whole class discussion with chart paper or whiteboard to record children's ideas.

◆ Open-ended questions: *"What are the creative arts?"* Or *"What are the arts?"* Follow-up response – *"Tell me more, or tell me about it. What else can you tell me?"*

◆ Discussion: Once children begin to share their ideas on what are the creative arts, generate discussion by asking probing questions encouraging more sharing and reflection. Record on chart paper or whiteboard what the children are saying.

◆ Review: Once you sense the children are ready to move on or have exhausted the list, do a quick review with a bit of adding or re-stating if a contribution was not clear.

◆ Have ready different stations for the different creative arts you want to introduce at this time. Example: Visual Arts: different materials, mediums (paint, clay), paper, any supplies appropriate for the class to explore.

  ◆ To begin with, offer a couple of options for younger children. Older children can be offered a fuller range of options. Keep it simple to begin with.

◆ Allow children time to explore, experiment, and try different forms of the visual arts.

◆ When ready to wrap this segment up, share projects or a work-in-progress in the whole group or small groups.

## Save the Project

Record with camera/cell phone or video the process to share later on a website, with families, or others.

## Extension

◆ Develop the theme of creative arts and STEM.

◆ Create puppets, a mural, a song or poem, or music to share detailing a STEM topic of choice.

  ◆ Keep it relevant and of interest to your young learners.

◆ Whole class discussion: Review the first lesson segment introducing the creative arts. Review their responses and maybe take a few minutes to look over the projects created.

◆ STEM focus: Nature – class garden (this can be a flower garden, vegetable, or bird and butterfly garden).

◆ Open-ended question: *"How can we show our bird and butterfly garden project using the creative arts?"*
  ◆ Follow-up response: *"Tell me more."*
  ◆ Allow children to contribute ideas, suggestions, ways of doing this and chart the information for all to see.
  ◆ Read their ideas back to the children when you sense they are done.
  ◆ Get a consensus as to how the children would like to show the garden using one or two art forms.

◆ Possibilities: Create a story, poem, song, music, or a mural.
  ◆ Choose one or two art forms for this lesson.

◆ Depending on the age of the children, they can generate a list of supplies and materials needed to create a representation of the bird and butterfly garden.

## Project Choice

If you choose to make a mural and/or poem:

◆ Have a class discussion on what is in the mural:
  ◆ Colors, plants, animals.
  ◆ Assign or let each child choose what to create from the choices offered.

◆ The layout of the mural should be done in advance so children see where to put things.

◆ This part of the larger lesson requires organization, adult support, clear directions, and clear use of materials.

◆ Some children might want to work on the mural while others might want to work with a teacher on a poem, if doing a poem.
  ◆ Whole class poem.
  ◆ Small group set of poems.
  ◆ Individual poems for a class book of poems on the garden.

◆ How you choose to set these two activities up will reflect on your schedule, setting and space, materials, and your students.

◆ This project can take a while to complete, depending on how much time is given to it and student interest.

◆ Record process with video and/or photos to share with the community of others (family, other classes, website, bulletin board).

◆ When it is completed, celebrate the accomplishment and share with others. Give children an opportunity to talk about their process and how they went about doing their part of the project.

## Conclusion

◆ Revisit the process and discussions. Read over what children discussed and decided on for the project(s) and their interpretation of the creative arts.
   ◆ Did they meet the goals of the project and their own plans?
◆ Assessment: Were all the children engaged?
◆ Were all the children able to participate?
◆ Developmentally Appropriate Practice tie-in:
   ◆ Families: Reach out to families prior to the lessons to see if there are any experts or resources. Also let the families know what their child will be doing in class for a few days.
   ◆ Intentional teaching: thoughtful, child-centric, open-ended questions, support all learners where they are developmentally.

# 3

# Science in Early Childhood Education

## Introduction

Science is the study of the physical and natural world through observation, experimentation, and theoretical investigation or modeling, in order to categorize and understand the behavior of all things. Science is what children intuitively do – they study the physical and natural world through observation while exploring the nature of objects and events through experimentation. Knowledge is built through observation and experiments and is hierarchically organized within our brains as we grow and learn more through our interactions with the natural and physical world.

Children spend their days engaged in observations and hands-on activities where they then construct ideas and beliefs about their world as a result of these personal experiences. Using their senses along with their ability to move and manipulate objects, children build a hierarchical belief system to understand, predict, and organize their experiences in the world, and ultimately their understanding of the environment around them. How can we as teachers connect what children naturally do to the more systematic scientific process of inquiry and investigation into the natural and physical world?

DOI: 10.4324/9781003395614-3

Children's experiences are influenced by home and community settings, and those living within those settings. Family, friends, neighbors, caregivers, childcare facilities, social context, and cultural norms of family influence a child's first experiences and perceptions of life. Their prior knowledge originates from these early experiences. This in turn forms the way each child interprets and understands the world around them.

To provide meaningful learning experiences, we work to develop an appreciation within the young child for how science concepts both connect with and impact each of us individually and within the larger context of our world. To help young children begin this journey of awareness and appreciation, start small with simple observations which come from daily events or activities. Using meaningful questions, direct the child's attention to observable changes or characteristics of an object or event in their immediate environment. Work to first create connections between the child and the child's world, and then expand those connections out into the larger world.

Use children's innate curiosity about their world as a springboard for activities that develop scientific language and other cognitive skills. Science investigations involve children asking questions, looking for answers, conducting investigations, and collecting data.

To help young children experience science in this context, we as engaged adults and caregivers observe their activities, ask probing questions of the child, and encourage the child to ask questions of their own. "Discovery learning" puts the child at the center of the inquiry process. As noted in Chapter 1, this type of child-centric learning can lead to continued misconceptions or naïve (unrefined) understandings unless an adult participates and is present to offer insights and thoughtful questions guiding the child in his/her inquiry and discovery. To make the inquiry interesting (and to hook their attention), it must be meaningful to the child.

Children construct understanding based on experience and prior knowledge. Take children's own knowledge as a starting point, realizing that this "knowledge" is also a belief system based on experience. Asking meaningful questions encourages the child to think and reflect in ways that yes/no questions can miss.

Integrate science daily into the classroom and throughout the academic year. An integrated focus is built over time using topics of interest and relevance to the children. Topics such as trees, seasons, sky, stars, moon, plants, animals, rocks, and changes, to name just a few, are appropriate for scientific investigations by young children. Take your cue from their lives and interests.

## How Young Children Learn Science and Ways Educators Can Support Them

How young children view the world and come to understand it develops over time and with experience. We know that children's reasoning capabilities develop across the early years. Young children take in new information through observation and experience, and then construct new understandings as long as they have a foundation upon which to build their new understandings or cognitive building blocks. Concept maps (see Chapter 1) show the way a child thinks about a specific concept. Once again, I stress the importance of prior knowledge – what the child already "knows." As Loveless concluded in a 2021 paper, "Studies of interventions that simply ratchet up expectations without regard for students' prior knowledge have yielded disappointing results" (Loveless, 2021).

Conceptual learning and knowledge (involving principles, ideas, and other concepts) are an integral part of a child's learning journey. This type of learning builds upon what a child already knows in order to develop a deeper appreciation and understanding, while relating one idea or concept to another. Leveraging prior knowledge, or what a child already knows (or believes to be valid), is the key to meaningful learning.

The language of science – inquiry and investigation – grows as children gain conceptual knowledge or understanding of the concepts. Bring science into your classroom throughout the school year. Integrate it into daily routines modeling the language and principles of inquiry and investigation. Using this approach will become familiar and more understandable over time as children experience them regularly in the classroom. Allow the daily class routine to embrace the notions of inquiry and investigation. Make science part of each day instead of focusing on a unit on science offered once or twice a year. Observations, data collection, experiments, modeling, comparisons, analysis, predictions, patterns, changes over time, and sorting, and classifying are just a few activities which utilize and encourage the language of science and provide opportunities for inquiry and investigation.

Let young children learn science through active involvement with first-hand investigative experiences. Involve them in the "doing" of science rather than learning scientific facts as presented by others. As children interact with their environment, whether it is the classroom, outside, or their home, they should be engaged both physically and cognitively in their investigations as much as possible. Science taught or experienced in this fashion becomes a way of thinking and working to understand the world.

Encourage children to discover or construct their own ideas. Developing new concepts or ideas is an active process and usually begins with a child-centered inquiry focusing on the asking of questions by the child. Teachers can pose additional questions which are relevant to the child's own interests. A give and take can take place, of questions and inquiry between the child, teacher, or others. Knowing the "right answer" is not one of the primary objectives of science in the early childhood curriculum. A far more important objective is to help children realize that many answers about the world can be discovered through their own investigations. Science exploration involves coming up with ideas of one's own.

## Constructivism and Its Role in the Science Classroom

Constructivism is the idea whereby each learner's prior knowledge provides the lens through which all new learning occurs (is constructed), including classroom instruction. A constructivist approach to education is based on the understanding that knowledge is constructed by children versus being given to them. As children interact with the world around them, they develop their own complex and varying theories about this world.

An example of this approach can be the following: In the block area of the classroom, a child constructs a tower. She uses a little block for the foundation and places much larger blocks on top of the small one. The tower does not stay up for long, it tumbles down and the young builder wonders why. During her construction, a teacher has been observing her efforts and comes over to chat asking what happened and then wondering why the tower tumbled down. The young builder reflects, and tries again with support and encouragement from the teacher to help her think and experiment with different blocks. Through her experiences and hands-on work with the blocks, the young builder is constructing understanding of the nature and behavior of different types of blocks. She is helped in this investigation and exploration with meaningful questions posed by her teacher.

When working from a constructivist approach, you as the teacher provide a supportive environment where your learners are encouraged to go about testing and revising their theories. Key ingredients for a supportive environment include a variety of interesting materials for children to explore and manipulate, unstructured time for children to develop and test their own ideas, and a social climate that tells the children that questions and experimentation are as valuable as knowing the right answers. Thoughtful and probing questions posed by the teacher at just the right time are also important to help children construct their own understandings.

Most children have difficulty constructing understanding simply by engaging in an activity. For our example of the block builder, if the teacher had not interacted with support and the use of thoughtful questions, the child might have continued using only small blocks for her base and keep wondering why her tower does not stay up to the point of frustration. Use probing and meaningful questions to provide a bridge between what the child already knows and what they experience through an activity takes a student forward in their thinking.

We interpret the world that we experience and give it meaning grounded in our prior experience. Children are typically constructing knowledge regardless of whether the context supports a constructivist perspective or not.

## Knowledge to Practice: How Do We Get from Here to There?

Children's innate curiosity about their world can be used as a springboard for activities that develop scientific language – inquiry and investigation – and other cognitive skills. Centering an investigation on a topic or theme of interest to children engages their natural curiosity in addition to connecting with their prior knowledge. Using both the *Next Generation Science Standards Practices* and *Crosscutting Concepts*, children can be guided in the development of scientific language supporting cognitive skills. A summary of some applicable Practices and Crosscutting Concepts appropriate for the early years is given below.

### Practices

Practices are the methods scientists and engineers use as they explore, experiment, test, and investigate theories about the world.

- *Asking questions (science) and defining problems (engineering):*
    - Science is what children do – they ask questions, which is also what good scientists do. Scientists pursue questions that have already been asked and identify new questions that build on prior knowledge.
    - Engineering typically begins with a problem, need, or interest requiring a solution.
- *Constructing explanations (science) and designing solutions (engineering):*
    - Children generally have explanations for why certain events occurred. Guiding them in their explanations with thoughtful questions from the teacher helps the young investigator reflect and ponder.
    - Designing solutions in engineering for the young builder includes determining the problem, proposing a solution, testing it out, redesigning, testing, with

more adjustments as needed. This process begins to lay down the framework for later more complex engineering problems and solutions.

♦ *Planning and carrying out investigations*: This practice is an important one scientists use to address their questions. Scientists strive to keep their investigation objective and free of bias as they go about addressing their questions. This practice is also important to convey to the child planning an investigation. Young children can often plan and carry out simple investigations stemming from a question of their own. Using meaningful questions as ways to guide how an answer might be found will inform and direct the child's methods and plan. In addition, help the child develop an awareness of expectations and/or bias as they anticipate the outcome of their investigation. "Bias" can refer to designing an investigation or study that may deliberately or inadvertently favor a certain outcome.

♦ *Analyzing and interpreting data*: Following an investigation, information or data will have been generated. Help young children look over the data or results of an investigation to determine if their question has been answered and what they learned from this process. Scientists and engineers alike analyze data to ascertain if their study or other designs have addressed the problem.

♦ *Obtaining, evaluating, and communicating information*: Sharing outcomes and observed results from projects, experiments, and trials is a significant practice of scientists and engineers.

## Crosscutting Concepts

These concepts apply across all the domains of science. They connect ways scientists examine, think about, and understand the different science disciplines.

♦ *Patterns*: Patterns are everywhere in our lives. These can be used to organize and classify information, they inform us about behaviors, they help us predict and understand, and they are tied to all disciplines of STEAM.

- *Cause and effect*: Young children characteristically want to know why something happened. Examining the progression of events leading up to the final one lays the foundation for later and more detailed investigations into the chain of interactions which resulted in one outcome over another. Meaningful questions from the teacher can guide the young investigator along the trajectory of events possibly arriving at an understanding or solution.
- *Structure and function*: This crosscutting concept creates connections between how an organism or object functions and the structural mechanisms that allow that function to occur. This concept also provides an opportunity to develop observational skills about form and function.
- *Stability and change*: Children have the ability to take in how things change or stay the same. With exploration, experimentation, observation, and discussion, young learners can begin to develop a sense of what it means to change or to remain stable. Change is an integral part of their lives, helping them to identify this concept will help them as they observe their world over time.

## Science: Life Sciences, Physical Sciences, Earth and Space Sciences

**When Skies Are Low and Days Are Dark**
*N. M. Bodecker*

When the skies are low
And days are dark,
And frost bites
Like a hungry shark,
When mufflers muffle
Ears and nose,
And puffy sparrows
Huddle close-
How nice to know
That February

Is something purely
Temporary.

The sciences are an exciting place to begin investigative adventures with young children. In this chapter we first explore the life sciences, then we delve into the physical sciences of chemistry and physics, and finally we touch on the Earth's place in the universe, a process which takes us from *terra firma* out to our solar system and the universe. This last area of study is a complex one requiring abstract thought. It is good to introduce this type of study in concept at an early age but also to save an in-depth treatment of it for when children are able to grasp the complexities of the universe and our solar system in later years.

## Life Sciences

How thrilling to explore all that is life on Earth. The realm of "life sciences" covers the structure and function of all organisms – from microbes to plants to animals – their ecosystems (where organisms live), and how they interact with each other and with their habitat. The Next Generation Science Standards (NGSS) (8–9) summarize the core ideas in the life sciences in this way: "All organisms are related by evolution and that evolutionary processes have led to the tremendous diversity of the biosphere" (four specific core ideas are identified by NGSS as the principal ones relevant to life sciences). In the NGSS Life Sciences section, core ideas LS1 (From Molecules to Organisms: Structures and Processes) and LS2 (Ecosystems: Interactions, Energy, and Dynamics) are introduced in ways accessible to young children, while embedding key elements within rich areas of study: environmental education, playscapes, and a nature study.

### Environmental Education
In this section, teachers can be guided by the curriculum of the North American Association for Environmental Education (NAAEE) with a special focus on early childhood education.

## What Is Environmental Education?

In my experience, young children revel in being outside. There is a sense of freedom in exploring the outdoor space, which can be enhanced by the opportunities to experience nature and our environment. Environmental education seeks to show children the wonder of nature, while helping them to appreciate the variety of life forms inhabiting different areas, such as woods, fields, streams, oceans, backyards, and playgrounds. Being close to nature can bring a sense of wonder, and this sense can guide children to see how we are interconnected to the natural world. It is our goal as teachers to help children cultivate an awareness and sensitivity to the delicate balance of nature and our place within it.

The North American Association for Environmental Education's (NAAEE) guiding principles provide clear direction for the educator ready to delve into a rich and rewarding exploration of environmental education for young children. Being outside, regardless of where your classroom is located, is key to bringing the experience alive for young children. Bringing some aspect of the outside to the inside of the classroom also enhances the learning, especially if the outside is limited due to possible constraints of the setting and outside space.

## Key Aspects of Early Childhood Environmental Education

The NAAEE has detailed some key aspects of early childhood education as shown below (NAAEE, 2022):

- ◆ *Human well-being*: The well-being of humans is connected to the systems we create and live with – educational, political, social, cultures, technologies – and which ultimately impact our environment. We exist in a balance within rather than outside nature; the overall health of our environment and Earth systems can experience disruptions when the balance is disturbed. Because we exist interdependently with nature, our own well-being reflects and is reflected by the well-being of our Earth and its systems.

- *Importance of where one lives*: Learn about where we live, and what are the characteristics of our environment and our relationship to it.
- *Integration and infusion*: Bring environmental education into daily activities and experiences in the classroom and outside.
- *Justice, equity, diversity, and inclusion*: Teachers can promote equity throughout the teaching, learning, and research continuum within environmental education by helping their learners recognize that not all individuals, groups, communities, or cultures are able to equally experience the principles of fairness and justice, especially with respect to environmental stewardship. As proponents of environment education, teachers should stress that all people are entitled to equitable circumstances and opportunities, whereby the worth and dignity of all are embraced.
- *Lifelong learning*: Foster an ongoing relationship with nature through daily investigations, supporting creative exploration, and problem-solving, which help support lifelong learning.
- *Roots in the real world*: Introduce your students to the materials available within your outside setting. Dig, sort, identify, organize, group, and find patterns. Help children become knowledgeable and comfortable with nature and the world outside.
- *Sustainable future*: NAAEE has committed to supporting the United Nations Sustainable Development Goals as a key principle. This key principle looks to the future acknowledging the responsibility of each individual's choices which ultimately affect our global environment.
- *Systems and systems thinking*: Help students learn about and recognize systems, which are a group of related items that form a whole, such as a family or a community of neighbors, plants or animals.

There are many possibilities for investigation and inquiry within the key aspects of NAAEE's guiding principles. The next topic we explore within the context of life science and environmental education is that of *playscapes*. Playscapes are a form of playground with a focus on children engaging in the natural environment. This focus may not be provided for in many of the playgrounds we are familiar with or have experienced with our young students (and perhaps our children or during our own childhoods).

## Playscapes

All natural playgrounds, or playscapes are dedicated spaces for children to play within an engaging outdoor environment that reflects the local landscape. They have become a topic of interest to many as evidenced by the number of nature education books on the market, but these initiatives and similar grass roots efforts in the US typically need to grow in proportion to the population of young children who would benefit from access to such natural playgrounds. Carr and Luken (2014, pp. 30–31) propose the following lists for playscape principles and features.

Playscape principles:

1. Playscapes elicit hands-on, multi-sensory, unique and personal experiences for children.
2. Nature is the focus, not man-made materials.
3. Areas within the playscape are designed to be open-ended with multiple and divergent uses.
4. Materials and spaces are not designed to be used in predetermined ways.
5. Selected playscape plants and materials are ones that can be found in nature, preferably indigenous to the local landscape.
6. Playscape materials provide opportunities to be touched, manipulated, dug, moved, picked, dammed, climbed, built, and experienced by children as they choose to do so.
7. Playscapes are built to encourage risk-taking, investigation, language, sensory experiences.

Playscape features:

1. Accessible water – streams, fountains, wading ponds
2. Non-level topography
3. Gardens and/or edible landscape materials
4. Sand, rocks, boulders
5. Trees, grasses, shrubs, flowers, herbs, etc.
6. Nature-themed art or some play equipment may be included, but should not intrude upon or dominate the playscape.
7. Pathways and gathering spaces
8. Hiding places, tunnels, felled logs, and digging pits
9. Seating for adults to observe children's play
10. Storage for child-sized equipment (shovels, buckets, etc.).

## Nature Study: Making It Happen in Your Classroom

Making nature study happen in your classroom is not as hard as you might think. Find ways to fit it into the weekly schedule. Locate an outdoor spot for regular visits and observations. Being in the outdoors, regardless of where your outdoors is located, requires certain safety measures to be part of the experience. Your setting, the children, and your community will inform your needs and safety choices. Identify nature study resources within your community – know who your experts are, line up volunteers for outings and for help in the classroom, and find organizations within your school and community that are nature-oriented and can provide materials, space, time, and guides. Familiarize yourself with the tools and supplies that will be needed for your explorations. Containers with screw-on lids, spades, or scoops, bags, buckets, sieves, baggies, hand-held magnifying glasses, and gloves are some of what you might want to consider bringing along. The choice of tools and supplies will naturally depend on your specific goal for each outing. Nature journals are an important part of your explorations, nature study, and learning processes. Children can draw what they see or remember, photos can be used, or others can write for a child if that is not appropriate for your students. Also, magazines can provide images to be used in nature journals. Your "nature rambles" and inquiries can be enhanced and developed through the use of thoughtful and meaningful questions. Make them open-ended and focus attention on the details while supporting new thinking and conceptual growth – notice, pause, and record. Finally, as a summative activity for your whole class, share observations while recording them on chart paper or a digital device such as a whiteboard. If using chart paper, these collections of observations can be displayed around the room, providing something which children can revisit while building their understandings, experiences, and the language of nature studies.

Nature studies can focus on a host of specific topics, or a can be a general observational exercise. If doing a specific nature study, know what your students will encounter on your study, including types of plants and animals, and what the environment will be like. Then, determine a specific focus for your excursion out into the outdoors. It could be to look closely at the different plants, where they are located – in the shade, sunlight, near water, or not. Are the plants tall or short? What grows near certain plants? If you are venturing into a forest setting, look closely at the forest floor and the many different animals and plants which will be found there. Begin to group the different plants and animals into categories depending on the different attributes. Determine in advance the list of plant and animal attributes. This helps children organize, categorize, and group their observations. The different characteristics of the environment can be noted and then organized into categories. Grouping attributes whether it is for plants, animals, or the setting, is determined by which features are chosen to focus on. For instance, will you focus on where plants are located, or the type of plant or the size of the plant? Training your students to become observers of details is an ongoing exercise, one which will last well into adulthood but with a nature study program, it can begin in the early years.

Noticing the different parts of plants and animals (to a practical extent) is an integral component of life sciences and reflects the NGSS LS1 principle. Structure and function become apparent as students examine the parts of different plants encountered in our walks outside. Plants have roots, leaves, stems, many have flowers, and in the fall they have seeds. How do these plant parts help with survival? What do plants and animals need to survive? Food, shelter, and protection from predators or other plants and animals are all essential for the survival of most forms of life, but different organisms acquire and utilize these things in different ways. Help your young naturalists begin to use specific vocabulary for identifying and naming plants and animals found in nature. Instead of a generic reference to "bugs," name the animal encountered as beetle, bee, or ant (for example). Use the vocabulary of plant anatomy, for instance, roots, stems, leaves, flowers, seeds, and fruit. Look closely at plants and animals found along the way on the nature study.

The change of seasons (where applicable) can also provide a focus for your nature study. Observing what happens throughout the year ties into structure and function – plants and animals change how they look and their behavior over the course of the seasons. The environment you have available to you determines much about your nature excursions and what you will see and encounter. Remember to choose a topic of interest and relevancy to your students.

## Practices
♦ Asking questions
♦ Planning and carrying out investigations
♦ Constructing explanations
♦ Engaging in argument from evidence
♦ Obtaining, evaluating, and communicating information.

## Crosscutting Concepts
♦ Patterns
♦ Cause and effect
♦ Structure and function
♦ Stability and change.

See Table 3.1 for Life Science Activities.

**TABLE 3.1** Life Science activities

| Science: life sciences | Activities and creative arts |
| --- | --- |
| Environmental Education | Spending time outside – looking, listening, touching (with care), smelling, tasting as appropriate |
| | Take pictures of nature |
| | Collecting items (as appropriate) for collages, murals, paintings, journals, sorting and classifying |
| | Share songs about the outdoors and nature |
| | Re-create sounds in nature with musical instruments |
| | Explore movement in nature (wind, rain, storms, waves) through creative movement |
| | Learn about where we live, the characteristics of our environment: create a mural, individual drawings or paintings, class poem |
| | Bring the outdoors into the daily experiences of the children. |
| Playscapes | Areas in the playscape can contain activities and materials for children to explore and experiment with: water, sand, and other objects which can be used for different purposes |
| | Have within the playscape items which can be moved creating spaces for different types of imaginative play |
| | In the classroom children can re-create favorite spaces in the playscape with art or using a journal write (if appropriate) or illustrate favorite spaces or activities |
| Nature Study | Make it a regular part of the curriculum and schedule |
| | There are many choices to explore for a nature study, choose one or more which is of interest to your students and is appropriate for your time, space, and setting |
| | Creative arts dovetails well with a nature study |
| | Songs, poems, stories, art, music, drama/puppets all pair with your nature study |
| | School gardens: journals, paintings, data collecting, cycles, mural, songs about gardens and growing, filming and photography to record events and progress, poetry – a class poem or short story about the garden, its progress, and the class work on it. |
| | Share all art projects with the school community, families, and the larger community. |

# Physical Sciences and Their Place in the Early Childhood Classroom

Physical sciences include chemistry and physics among other core ideas. In this section we focus on forces and motion and on chemical reactions. These topics are inherent in the study of chemistry and physics – disciplines which are not always associated with the early childhood classroom, but which nevertheless are ever-present as observable phenomena. Young children can recognize these events without labeling them as physics or chemistry per se, and they begin to think about them and ask questions. Our work is to help them by asking meaningful questions about their observations and experiences, a process which then lays the foundation for future thinking and inquiry in these two areas.

What is physical science, what are chemical reactions? Physical science and chemical reactions involve matter – something which occupies space and possesses mass – and its interactions. Reactions involving matter include mechanisms of cause and effect – you add heat to paper and it burns (chemical change), or you put water in the freezer and ice forms (physical change). Winter arrives seasonally in many areas of the US and if it is cold enough with a certain amount of atmospheric moisture, we get snow (physical change). Children's innate curiosity for these things can drive investigations and inquiry into the physical sciences.

**Winter Morning**
*Ogden Nash*

Winter is the king of showmen,
Turning tree stumps into snow men
And houses into birthday cakes
And spreading sugar over lakes.
Smooth and clean and frosty white,
The world looks good enough to bite.
That's the season to be young,

Catching snowflakes on your tongue.
Snow is snow when it's snowing,
And I'm sorry it's slushy when its going.

"*Winter Morning*" is a fun poem in which to begin a study of physical sciences focusing on change, and cause and effect. This poem invites the reader and listener to imagine a world changed through a blanket of snow and how our perceptions change in response to what we see around us outside. The language of the poem invites word play – showmen/snow men; cakes/lakes; white/bite; young/tongue; snowing/going. "Winter Morning" paints a picture of a snowy world turned slushy which opens discussion as to change and cause and effect. Warm temperatures and cold ones create change over time.

## Practices

Many of the practices are integrated in this simple poem, *Winter Morning*. Asking questions, constructing explanations, engaging in argument from evidence, and obtaining, evaluating, and communicating ideas can be activated through this poem. Some of the practices might need hands-on explorations which are possible if you live in areas of snow and cold.

◆ *Asking questions*: Asking meaningful questions of the children and encourage questions from them, for example what patterns they noticed, or what change occurred throughout the poem. What do they know about snowflakes? What is their experience with snowy days or days when the snow begins to melt? The young child can respond to thoughtful questions about snowflakes from the poem and from their personal experience, if applicable. Use of additional images of snow and snowflakes provide the learners with information helping them develop questions of their own: What is snow? How is snow made? Can it be made in the classroom, like making ice (using the freezer of a refrigerator)?

◆ *Constructing explanations*: Sharing an explanation does not necessarily mean that it is the correct or sole valid one, but it is one the young learner has constructed using his/her prior knowledge and experience. In response to a question from the teacher specifically asking about what is observed, the student comes up with his/her own explanation in response to the question.

♦ *Engaging in argument from evidence*: Using observed information, the child can be able to construct an argument to explain what is happening or why.

♦ *Obtaining, evaluating, and communicating ideas*: Collect information from observations, respond to questions about the specific information; share insights with others about the conclusions of the young learner.

## Crosscutting Concepts

♦ *Patterns*: Noticing patterns is a first step toward organizing information in our natural world. We classify through noticing and grouping similarities and differences. Once patterns begin to be noticed, children can be guided in ways to recognize, group, and record observed patterns.

  ♦ *Noticing variation*: How are things the same or different (similarities may be easier to identify than differences)?

  ♦ *Poem patterns*: seasons: winter into spring, words in the poem: showmen/snow men; cakes/lakes; white/bite; young/tongue; snowing/going.

♦ *Cause and effect*: How do organisms respond to changing environments? In the poem we notice that weather outcomes (cause) determine clothing choices (effect). We respond to cold weather by wearing warm clothes, and/or more clothing items (such as mittens and hats) than we do when the weather is warm.

♦ *Structure and function*: In the winter, tree shape (evergreen and deciduous) allows the tree to survive in a snowy environment. Deciduous trees typically lose their leaves, otherwise the leaves would be like platforms for the snow to land on, causing possible damage to the tree. The evergreen has thin needles instead of leaves which allow the snow to slip off without causing damage to the tree.

◆ *Stability and change*: At the end of the poem the snow becomes slushy. This typically occurs when the temperature warms up. Snow arrives in the winter season when it is cold, and melts or becomes slushy with the arrival of warmer temperatures, usually when spring arrives.

# Chemistry

It might seem far-fetched to include chemistry in the early childhood classroom, but the language of chemical change, ways of thinking, and the exciting activities involving chemistry justify its place in the early childhood setting. The following section on chemistry presents an overview of its key characteristics with language useful to both teacher and student.

Chemistry is investigating the different properties of substances and changes they undergo through specific interactions, such as our paper and heat example. There are four states of matter: solid, liquid, gas, and plasma. Matter has properties of varying degrees of hardness and conductivity. It is important to note that changes accompanying matter fall into one of two categories: physical change or chemical change. Burning paper results in a chemical change – it cannot be reconstructed as paper because it has been changed into substances that are not paper. Adding heat to ice creates a change in the ice; it becomes water. If that water is exposed to below-freezing temperatures, it forms ice. This "phase change," like boiling water into steam, is a process which can be reversed, therefore, it is a physical change. There are many hands-on activities for children to explore involving both physical changes and chemical changes – cooking is a great activity in which to explore some of these characteristics.

## Matter and Its Interactions
◆ *States of matter*: Solid, liquid, gas, or plasma
◆ *Properties*: Hardness, conductivity. There are many others, like color, form (crystalline, lattice, etc.), magnetic property, solubility, density/specific gravity, etc.

**TABLE 3.2** Asking meaningful questions: chemistry

| Actions | Questions |
| --- | --- |
| Remember: identify, name, repeat, recall | What materials are you using? |
| Understand: describe, discuss, explain, summarize | What do you think will happen when you mix these two liquids? Follow-up: What happened when you did mix them? |
| Apply: explain why, dramatize, identify with/relate to | Where else have you seen these liquids? |
| Analyze: recognize change, experiment, infer, compare, contrast | What might make the experiment have a different outcome? |
| Evaluate: express opinion, judge, defend/criticize | Why did the liquid turn that color (or behave in that manner?) Do you think this result represents a physical or chemical change? |
| Create: make, construct, design, author | Can you create your own liquid experiment? |

◆ *Reactions*
   ◆ A physical change in a substance doesn't change the substance's constituent parts, for example, ice to water and water to ice, water to steam/steam to water.
   ◆ A chemical change is where there is a chemical reaction. The molecular structure is changed, thereby resulting in a new substance, for example, paper is burned, it changes into different substances that are not paper: carbon dioxide ($CO_2$), water vapor, and ash.

Table 3.2 summarizes some ways to ask questions of a simple chemistry experiment involving mixing of two different liquids as a chemistry example (for instance, mixing two equal volumes of water colored blue and yellow with food coloring).

## Physics: Forces and Motion

Movement is a constant in the early childhood classroom. Children move in different ways and directions sometimes avoiding other objects such as classmates (or sometimes not). When two objects meet, such as two children, reactions can be instant and often unforeseen by the child or children.

Even young children love to experiment with gravity and motion, dropping items, such as a cup, a ball, or toy onto the floor from some height (the hand, or even the highchair) for the delight of it. Children are engaged with the interactions of objects when they push objects off tables, drop balls to see what happens next, or build tall block structures only to knock them down. In doing these things, they are consciously or unconsciously investigating and experimenting with forces and motion.

This section introduces a curriculum developed by DeVries and Sales (2011) built on principles of physics and a constructivist approach to teaching and learning. The basic precepts presented here are simple yet involve complex experiences supported by hands-on activities, careful organization of materials, space, and time, along with meaningful questions asked by the teacher – you. These activities can be used with most early childhood ages, from pre-school on up.

## Constructivism in the Physics Classroom

Constructing our own understanding of events – actions and reactions – using our prior knowledge of ways things behave is constructivism in action. As noted previously in this book, constructivism leverages learning experiences on an active rather than passive basis, and builds on what learners believe they already understand about something. This approach in the classroom can be implemented with young children to promote a meaningful learning experience.

For students to construct meaningful understanding, the learning context needs to be placed within genuine instructional activities. Providing young learners with a real-life context for their scientific experience can allow them to apply their prior knowledge within the classroom setting and, with guidance from the teacher, work through emerging understanding (Merrill, 2012).

*Ramps & Pathways* is a curriculum developed by Rheta DeVries and Christina Sales at the University of Northern Iowa (UNI). It takes a constructionist perspective about children's learning, and embeds a physics-oriented approach within that learning model. The "ramps" and "pathways" are comprised of inclined or flat sections of tracks. Various objects are placed at different locations along the pathways or ramps, and their movements along the tracks are predicted and observed, after which outcomes are explained using student-developed theories. Children's misconceptions about how this particular model works can be revealed as they test different theories and ways of implementing slope, different types of supports, a variety of objects to travel the pathways, types of connections, targets, and pathway designs (DeVries & Sales, 2011). Each aspect of building, experimenting, predicting, and then observing the outcome supports a constructivist learning experience. Children experiment with different objects to go along the ramps and pathways. The tracks are set up in a myriad of different arrangements supporting constructivist thinking and learning. The teachers' approach with children should be one of cooperation rather than coercion, which means teachers should refrain from directing actions or choices, but instead support the learner's own experience through asking meaningful questions about design choices. Children can also work cooperatively with peers to organize their building projects to test a hypothesis regarding objects' behaviors as a function of organization of tracks.

Ramps and pathways activities encourage children in the construction of practical knowledge through hands-on activities. As always, children's work should be supported by teachers asking meaningful and probing questions which help the child think in different and new ways about their experiences and observations.

Ramps and pathways-type explorations will require materials, space, and time. Plan ahead so you are able to accommodate this exciting inquiry experience. As you can imagine, setting ramps and other tracks up in the classroom will require a lot of territory. If possible, plan for your ramps and pathways activity to span more than a day. Materials that DeVries and Sales have found to work best are cove moldings 1¾ inches wide cut into lengths of 1, 2, 3, and 4 feet. Things to test out and try on

**TABLE 3.3** Asking meaningful questions: physics: ramps and pathways

| Actions | Questions |
| --- | --- |
| Remember: identify, name, repeat, recall | What materials are you using? |
| Understand: describe, discuss, explain, summarize | I noticed you placed that at the end of your pathway. Why? |
| Apply: explain why, dramatize, identify with/relate to | Can you explain why you chose to angle your slope in that way? |
| Analyze: recognize change, experiment, infer, compare, contrast | Compare the object's movement between two pathways you can create |
| Evaluate: express opinion, judge, defend/criticize | Did the outcome meet your expectations? Why? |
| Create: make, construct, design, author | How would you create a series of ramps and pathways different from your current design? |

the tracks are an important element of the constructivist work of your children, in addition to the ramps and pathways design. Enjoy ramps and pathways with your students; it is inquiry and exploration at its best!

See Table 3.3 for examples of meaningful questions for Physics: Ramps and Pathways.

## Developmentally Appropriate Practice in the Science Classroom

◆ *Be intentional*: Decisions about how and what science is experienced in the classroom should match both the children's interests and developmental levels, and be clearly planned.

◆ *The community of learners* is central to the science experiences. Teachers learn about each child so that science activities reflect the children's interests and abilities.

◆ *Development and learning* are enhanced through teaching strategies and methods. Science activities can be presented in many different ways, allowing children to experience them using multi-modalities (hands-on, visual, auditory, interactive, digital). Teachers should model, show, assess, and then revise if needed, ask meaningful questions, listen carefully, and provide clear directions.

◆ *Appropriate curriculum planning is important*: Know your science and developmental goals before creating your lessons.

◆ *Reciprocal relationships with families*: Build in opportunities for families to become involved in the children's experiences with different types of science.

◆ *Scaffold learning*: Provide relevant and/or individual support when and where it is needed as it is needed.

◆ *Constructivist learning*: Offer constructivist learning experiences throughout the day and build them within the curriculum. Offer different learning situations, such as whole group, small group, one-on-one, and learning centers. Teaching and learning conditions should vary as the way children learn best varies.

See Figure 3.1 for a concept map delineating the process of constructivist-based learning leading to conceptual change in the learner.

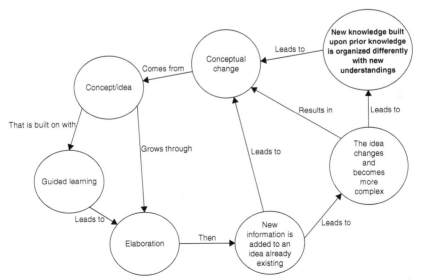

Figure 3.1  Concept map: process of constructivist-based learning leading to conceptual change in a learner.

This concept map is hierarchical in nature with a circular pathway of experience, learning, and understanding. The learner's foundation of prior knowledge is built upon through hands-on experiences. The connecting lines with arrows show the linking pathway which occurs when the learner's prior knowledge, which provides the stepping-off platform for new information and experiences, can challenge prior concepts. This new information, through hands-on opportunities, helps construct new ways of thinking about an observed or experienced event. The linking words placed on the arrows describe the way one concept impacts and changes the next concept linked to it.

See Table 3.4 for examples of activities for physical science.

## Exploring Earth and Space Science

### Taking Turns
*Norma Farber*

When sun goes home
Behind the trees,
And locks her shutters tight-
Then silver stars come out
With silver keys
To open up the night.

This section of the Sciences has many exciting and important content areas for young children to be introduced to for inquiry and investigations. Some of the areas for exploration are appropriate for in-depth inquiry and investigation, whereas other content can be brought in as an introduction with greater attention given to it in later grades.

The Earth and Space Science (ESS) content is complex and interdisciplinary in nature, including the domains of astrophysics, geophysics, geochemistry, oceanography, and geobiology.[1] One underlying discipline for these different areas is geology – the identification, analysis, and mapping of rocks which is a cornerstone of ESS, and an exploration children love. Geology reflects

**TABLE 3.4** Physical Science activities

| Science | Activities and creative arts |
|---|---|
| Chemistry: chemical change or physical change | Cooking/baking: adding different ingredients to produce something new: any type of baking will typically produce a new product, e.g., cakes, cookies, cupcakes, bread, muffins |
| | Cooking/baking will change the items which cannot be reconstructed as the original items |
| | Discussion of what the students predict and observe – record their thoughts |
| | Relate chemistry to Art through mixing colors in different ways and with different types of paint |
| | Relate chemistry to engineering through building using different materials or objects to form a new item, e.g., using Legos of various types to build a house or other structure – the different individual parts can create a new whole, the new structure can be measured, weighed and described – it can also be deconstructed into its different parts – physical change has taken place |
| Physics: Force and Motion | Ramps and Pathways |
| | Hands-on explorations |
| | Testing objects' behaviors in response to different forces – toy cars, blocks, water/sand table, sandbox/ outside exploration |
| | Cooking – the result of force on certain cooking activities (whipping cream, making butter, kneading bread) |
| | Controlled experiments with student participation – predicting, testing and observing outcomes, explanation of observed results – heavy metal balls on a string hitting each other – (Newton's Cradle Balance Balls, Newton's Pendulum, for example) |
| | Relate physics to the Arts: Dance/movement exemplify force and motion – a moving object in space (a child running, dancing, skipping) across the floor until s/he meets another object: what happens next and why? |
| | Force and motion of musical instruments – strumming, hitting, shaking, rattling |
| | Force and motion in nature – wind, clouds, waves and water, sand, rocks |
| | Record, share, discuss with class |

the geosphere, one of Earth's systems which includes all the rocks and minerals. It provides an exciting range of inquiry and investigation activities integrating many of the crosscutting concepts and practices in addition to integration with the arts.

From the component ideas in NGSS' Earth and Space Sciences, I have identified ones suited for early childhood investigations. Some relevant ESS component ideas included here are the universe and its stars; Earth and the solar system; the roles of water in the Earth's surface processes; weather and climate; natural resources; and human impacts on Earth's systems. Many of these topics are a natural for young explorers, such as weather and the roles of water in the Earth's surface processes, while other areas are important as an introduction. The Earth and our solar system is an appropriate unit for introducing to young children, but saving an in-depth investigation into this core idea until a later grade is advisable. The concept of climate can be hard for young minds to grasp since it is not a static thing but rather one which can and does change over time. Human choices impacting our climate and the changes resulting from these things are complex and can bring up misconceptions and confusion. Climate-based studies or discussions can be introduced even to young children; but the context should be appropriately simplified to enable their desired effect of understanding; more in-depth climate studies are best saved for curricula involving older children.

Having some background knowledge in the content area being explored helps ground us as teachers as we explore along with our young investigators. It does not mean we need to be experts; but having some of the language, an awareness of the systems involved, and how they interact with each other – along with an appreciation for the complexity of earth and space science – provides us as educators with a foundation upon which to work.

The four "Earth systems" – the atmosphere, hydrosphere, geosphere, and biosphere[2] are interconnected and small changes in one part of the system can have large and sudden consequences in parts of other systems, or no effect at all (NGSS). Knowledge of the many systems' interactions and feedbacks helps us understand how the Earth changes over time. Earth is also part of a larger system – the solar system – which is a small part of one of the many galaxies in the universe.

The Earth's systems, which are processes driving Earth's conditions and its continual evolution, change over time. The role of water with respect to all of Earth's systems and surface processes is an important topic relevant to all children, making it an appropriate and interesting study.

Finally, there are many human impacts on Earth systems through our interactions and interconnectedness with these systems. The importance of this topic was highlighted in the NAAEE's Key Aspects mentioned earlier in this chapter. Focusing on our natural resources and what they are helps young children begin to develop an awareness of our relationship to our local environment and our world at large. Our impact on Earth is a challenging area for young children to explore. Focusing on the positive things that are happening, and how even small environmental initiatives can make a difference, are appropriate topics for young learners.

## Earth and Space Science Topics
- ◆ The Universe and its Stars
- ◆ Earth and the Solar System
- ◆ Earth Materials and Systems
- ◆ The Role of Water in the Earth's Surface Processes
- ◆ Weather and Climate
- ◆ Natural Resources
- ◆ Human Impacts on Earth's Systems

## Earth's Place in the Universe

### The Universe and Its Stars: Earth and the Solar System
This is a big and abstract topic for young children to grasp. Introducing the notion of our solar system and the larger concept of the universe gives students the beginning language and ideas which will be developed later as their experience and cognition grow. Regardless of where they may live, young children have awareness of changes in our day and seasons. Night arrives and with its end our day begins. Spring comes after winter with

summer following spring. Fall arrives heralding the coming of winter. Seasons, cycles, changes in weather and our accompanying behaviors are part of each child's personal experience which makes it relevant to their learning. Other observable cycles can be included in an introduction to Earth's place in the universe, such as tides for those living on the coast, moon phases, star and planet patterns. These things can be observed, described, and predicted.

## Practices
♦ Asking questions
♦ Constructing explanations.

## Crosscutting Concepts
♦ Patterns.

## Earth's Systems

The Earth is constantly changing. How this comes about, and why are questions young children most likely are not thinking or asking about at this time. As educators, we should understand that all Earth's processes are linked to energy flow and matter cycling within and among Earth's systems, and that energy originates from the sun and from the Earth's interior. Transfer of energy and the movements of matter can cause chemical and physical changes among Earth's materials and living organisms. It is helpful for teachers to have some background knowledge of these processes. This level of information is typically not within young children's cognitive scope to understand at this stage. It is sufficiently important to acknowledge that Earth's systems are dynamic and our weather and climate are driven by interactions of the geosphere (all the rocks/minerals that make up Earth), the hydrosphere (the total amount of water on the planet), and the atmosphere (the layers of gases surrounding the Earth – about 78 percent nitrogen, 21 percent oxygen, and 1 percent other gases) with inputs of energy from the sun (NGSS, 2013).

## Practices
♦ Asking questions
♦ Constructing explanations.

## Crosscutting Concepts

◆ Patterns.

This core idea of ESS is rich with content which is engaging to young children. It includes the study of water, weather, climate, and rocks which tell many stories about the history of the Earth and its formation. Water is an absorbing area of investigation which has relevance for all children. Water and the role of water in the Earth's surface systems form a big area to explore, but for young children it can be fascinating and fun. The changes water undergoes from ice to flowing water to steam (in some geysers and other geothermal scenarios) is one children often can relate to first-hand. The water cycle can be introduced (Figure 3.2), but some processes can be hard for young children to grasp. The many roles water plays in our lives and ways it influences our Earth present many topics for inquiry. Water as an economic resource (fishing, tourism, boating) and water as a powerhouse of life are just two possible topics for exploration.

Weather determines our course of action as we plan our day, our choice of clothing, and activities. Weather, which can be benign or dangerous, is a daily occurrence while climate is a more abstract concept. Like "weather," *climate* has become part of our daily lexicon; so introducing children to the notion and language of climate is appropriate.

Rocks are items found in abundance in most outside settings, and their study can provide hours of fascinating investigations for young children. The study of rocks can engage young scientists in the process of inquiry and investigation as their nature unfolds through our research. Different rocks form under specific conditions, which in turn can provide clues as to what happened in the Earth's past. Even the most mundane hunk of rock can reveal a story about our Earth's history.

*Seeing Science Through Art: Sky Tree* by Thomas Locker and Candace Christiansen (2001) is a book of a collection of paintings with accompanying text highlighting the cyclical changes of the seasons with a particular focus on one tree. The Spring painting with its 8-line narrative shows the tree beginning to emerge from the cold of Winter. Within those eight lines, water cycle, seasons, growing cycle of a tree, language, our sun's energy as it warms the air, earth, and the tree are all depicted. I recommend this book for exploration of these different topics.

## Practices
- ◆ Asking questions
- ◆ Plan and carry out investigation
- ◆ Construct explanations
- ◆ Engaging in argument from evidence
- ◆ Obtaining, evaluating, and communicating information,

## Crosscutting Concepts
- ◆ Patterns
- ◆ Cause and effect
- ◆ Stability and change.

## Researching Rocks

Young children are well-known rock collectors. Rocks can be found in various forms in most environments and each rock tells its own story along with the Earth's story of change. Collecting, sorting, grouping, identifying patterns, similarities, and differences are activities which engage and inform young learners about the nature of rocks. Activate their prior knowledge through thoughtful questioning – what do you know about rocks?, what is a rock?, what is sand?, what is a boulder (or a mountain?)? Probing questions like these can also reveal misconceptions, which then informs additional teaching.

There are many ways to learn about, explore, investigate, and compare rocks and sand in their various forms. A hands-on rock and sand study integrating exploration with different aspects of the arts and other STEM areas is a natural for this topic. For example, rock and sand collages, paintings, and sculptures along with music, song, and dance can be easily integrated into this exploration. Recognizing patterns, similarities and differences, counting, and creating sets are some examples which also support math skills. Outdoor explorations to locate different forms of rocks and sand facilitate environmental education. Make use of journals and digital cameras to record such events.

A study of rocks and sand can be an introductory exploration into the world of geology. Let children collect, compare, and contrast their findings with their own collections and with the findings of classmates. Different outside areas such as woods, fields, bodies of water, urban settings, parks, or playgrounds will reveal a range of rock types and formations which are unique to the environment. This also is a topic for inquiry and investigation. A research-focused study starts with a question and then is followed by an investigation to answer the question. Determining whether (or how thoroughly) the question has been answered is something for the young scientist to ponder. If so, then another question can be posed; if not, a plan to try again is developed. All of this occurs with the teacher's support and guidance through thoughtful questions and careful listening.

A study of rocks and sand generates many questions and observations from young learners. Set up your classroom to accommodate rock and sand collections, and provide ways of examining them with magnifying glasses or even microscopes; the findings can be organized into posters, and charts (or other forms of recording data). Teacher or class-based observations and thoughtful questions can encourage the investigator and support additional inquiry.

Students are able to engage in the Practices and Crosscutting Concepts listed below. Whether a study is undertaken as a whole class, small group, or by an individual, teachers should help learners develop a question or set of questions to investigate their field study into rocks.

## Practices
◆ Asking questions
◆ Plan and carry out investigation
◆ Construct explanations
◆ Engaging in argument from evidence
◆ Obtaining, evaluating, and communicating information.

## Crosscutting Concepts
◆ Patterns
◆ Cause and effect
◆ Stability and change.

# The Roles of Water in the Earth's Surface Systems

## Water: Land and Ocean

Children – and I – love the feel, look, movement, and playfulness of water exploration.

The study of water and its role in our lives is a fascinating and important one – after all, water covers about 71 percent of the Earth's surface and makes up about 60 percent of our bodies. It lays the foundation for more in-depth explorations in later years and builds a sensitivity and awareness of water's vital importance to our lives, and all life on Earth, through its roles in the Earth's surface systems.

Our explorations, inquiry, and investigations in this section include the many formations on land and sea where water collects, moves through, or percolates into. Our connection to water ties in with weather, climate, and human impacts on Earth systems.

The amount of salt dissolved in water categorizes it as "salt-water" (more than 3 percent salt), "brackish" (less than 3 percent salt but more than 0.05 percent salt), or "fresh" (less than 0.05 percent salt). Freshwater is typically found in glaciers, rivers, streams, wetlands, vernal pools, watersheds, lakes, ponds, and bogs. Most icebergs are also freshwater, even though they may be in the ocean. Brackish water sources are typically found at the transitional points of water where freshwater meets seawater, forming estuaries. Marshes or swamps can be either fresh or salt depending on their location, whether inland or coastal (Mitsch & Gosselink, 1993). Full-strength salt water is found in the oceans, inland seas, and in some lakes.

Introduce children to the concept of one ocean. "Earth has one big ocean with many features" (Ocean Literacy, 2015). It is the "defining physical feature on our Planet Earth" (Ocean Literacy, 2015). Water exists as a solid, liquid and gas (or vapor). It is able to move rocks and soil from one place to another. This ties in with the study of rocks and sand.

Once a focus for water inquiry and investigation has been chosen, there are many angles which can be taken. The role water plays in the lives of different plants and animals, the different environments where water is found, different types of water – salt, brackish, or fresh. Explore the different bodies of water found around our Earth, such as swamps, bogs, ponds, rivers, streams, lakes, and oceans (or the "one ocean"). The ways we as humans use and depend on water for so many of the things we do daily form an opportunity for inquiry while connecting with environmental education. "How many ways can water be used?" is an excellent starting point for discussion, and can include uses for recreation, commerce, power, travel, and artistic inspiration, among others.

The water cycle comes to mind when exploring the role of water in our earth surface systems. The water cycle is complex, with aspects of the process which are not visible to the naked eye (such as evaporation – the result of which is visible, but not the process). Figure 3.2 is from the National Oceanic and Atmospheric Administration website and provides a detailed illustration of the processes involved in the water cycle.

Our water sources are precious. Helping children inquire into and investigate ways we can care for these resources will inform and guide their ways of thinking about the roles water plays in local and global environments and our lives. Forms of pollution which may ultimately percolate and migrate to the ocean, along with the potentially detrimental impacts on the environment from human use, are an important topic in an

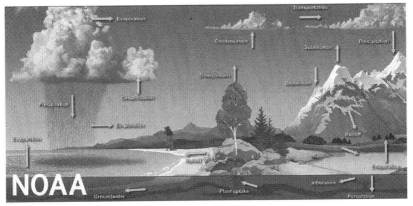

Figure 3.2 The water cycle.
Source: Dennis Cain/NWS, Image by NOAA.

investigation of water. It is important to be hopeful and non-judgmental as pollution is introduced to young children. The focus should be the ways we can help assess and counter the negative effects of human overuse and abuse, and the many ways we are caring for our environment currently (or might care in the future). Sharing success stories of waterways cleaned up from the effects of pollution provides a positive model for the power of human resourcefulness in combating negative effects on our water sources. For those in the New England area, *A River Ran Wild* by Lynne Cherry (2013) is an uplifting success story about the Nashua River which was declared "ecologically dead" in the 1960s. In 1965, the U.S. Congress passed the first Clean Water Act. In the following year, citizen initiatives led to the Massachusetts Clean Water Act of 1966. Through the work of a relative few, this river now runs clean and free.

An abundance of resources are available for research and to inspire, inform, extend the many different aspects of a study on the role of water in the Earth's surface systems. See Resources for additional information. Each state will likely have its own .gov resources for educational purposes.

## Practices
♦ Asking questions
♦ Plan and carry out investigation
♦ Construct explanations
♦ Engaging in argument from evidence
♦ Obtaining, evaluating, and communicating information.

## Crosscutting Concepts
♦ Patterns
♦ Cause and effect
♦ Stability and change.

# Weather and Climate

The next domain – weather and climate – ties in with our ocean studies. The NGSS says this about weather: "weather, which varies from day to day and seasonally throughout the year, is the condition of the atmosphere at a given place and time." The ocean exerts a major influence on our weather and ultimately our climate. It absorbs and stores large amounts of energy from the sun and releases it slowly. The ocean moderates and stabilizes global climates.

Use these guiding questions to discover what your young learners know: *What is weather? What do we know about it?* After introducing an area of investigation which taps into student interest and is relevant to their lives, access students' prior knowledge through direct questioning. Graph responses using the What I Know, What I Want to Learn, What I Learned (K-W-L) chart.

Young children will have misconceptions about weather which are varied and many. When misconceptions are revealed through direct questioning and class discussion, they can provide a valuable starting place for new information as long as the initial concept or misconception is carefully re-conceptualized with scaffolding and lots of hands-on experience and exposure.

Weather is a culturally rich domain infused with folklore, mythology, legends, and creator myths shared as stories, songs, dance, and art. It is a highly engaging study area where students can become immersed in the content. Weather is daily and impacts us always.

Climate, however, is a more challenging topic. The NGSS definition of climate is this: "Climate is longer term and location sensitive; it is the range of a region's weather over 1 year or many years, and, because it depends on latitude and geography, it varies from place to place." A climate is typically represented through and determined by weather data collected and averaged over a prolonged period of time, typically around 30 years. Recall that oceans exert a major influence on weather and climate. Large bodies of water absorb and store substantial amounts of energy from the sun and release it very slowly.

The study of climate poses certain challenges for young children. As NGSS states, climate is long-term, which in and of itself makes it a hard concept to grasp for the young learner. Introduce the concepts of climate (weather over time) and climate change using appropriate language so the child has some of the building blocks for forming the foundation for later explorations into those concepts.

The good news is that the world has made real progress in slowing down some types of climate change over the past few years. Solar and wind power, in many places of the world, are more available or economical than gas and coal or other "fossil fuels." Electric vehicles are becoming more affordable, and many governments are energetically funding clean energy.

See *Resources* for some of the organizations providing information online for climate and climate change. Check out your state .gov for additional information specific to your state and area.

## Practices

- ◆ Asking questions
- ◆ Plan and carry out investigation
- ◆ Construct explanations
- ◆ Engaging in argument from evidence
- ◆ Obtaining, evaluating, and communicating information,

## Crosscutting Concepts

- ◆ Patterns
- ◆ Cause and effect
- ◆ Stability and change.

# Earth and Human Activity

## Human Impact on Earth Systems

Treat this topic with care and sensitivity in order not to overwhelm young children with the many challenges our Earth faces from human impacts on all areas of our planet. Discuss ways children can make a difference, providing them with tools to counter damages and overuse while demonstrating good practices for our planet, such as recycling, growing gardens, and reducing waste. Also, as noted in the previous section, discuss what humans are doing to mitigate environmental and atmospheric damage. Resources from the previous two sections are useful and insightful when investigating this topic.

Explore with your investigators how we humans care for our natural resources and our environments and the ways we work to protect them, along with the plants and animals found there. Touch upon how we also use our natural resources in ways that might do harm to the plants and animals living in the particular habitat or particular environment. The natural home of an animal, plant or other organism is a habitat. "Environment" can be understood as the sum total of all the living and non-living elements within a particular given area. Living elements are animals and plants and some microbes, while non-living elements of the environment include rocks, water, land, sunlight, and air.

## Natural Resources

Most living things need oxygen, water, energy (made or consumed by the organism), and shelter (or a stable environment) in order to survive and thrive. "Survival" typically means being able to reproduce successfully, with healthy offspring able to themselves live and reproduce. Within our Earth's environment are ecosystems, which are "all of the organisms that live in a geographical area, together with the non-biological components that affect or exchange materials with the organisms (e.g. climate, energy, soil, nutrients)" (Freeman, 2002). The primary ecosystems are forest, grassland, desert, tundra, and fresh and salt water. The largest ecosystem on our planet can be represented through the "one ocean" concept mentioned earlier.

Natural resources are found within each ecosystem; these are used to support life and meet the needs of the organisms living in that system. Oil, coal, natural gas, metals, stone, sand, and forests are natural resources. Air, sunlight, soil, wind, different thermal environments, and water are also natural resources. Animals and plants found within each ecosystem can additionally be considered natural resources. How humans use the collective natural resources available to them determines many things about the scope and quality of our lives and our environment, which is the geographical area in which we live, encompassing all living and non-living things occurring naturally.

Humans' use and overuse of our natural resources have been a large area of concern and study for a long time. Helping young children understand what natural resources are, who needs them and how they are used is an introduction to this domain. Accessing their prior knowledge through asking thoughtful questions will inform the direction of the study. Families within your community might make their living through use of local natural resources. Those living near water – fresh or marine – might know (or be) lobstermen, fishermen, or people associated with an aquaculture business, such as growers or lab personnel working to ensure healthy aquaculture solutions to disease. Families may know specific scientists studying the effects of stressors on different natural resources located within a specific environment. We are all connected to and dependent upon natural resources. Recognizing our relationship to our environment and its natural resources begins the journey toward greater understanding and awareness of our interconnectivity. How we treat our natural resources impacts the quality of our lives and those who will come after in successive generations.

## Practices
- ◆ Asking questions
- ◆ Plan and carry out investigation
- ◆ Construct explanations
- ◆ Obtaining, evaluating, and communicating information
- ◆ Analyzing and interpreting data

## Crosscutting Concepts
- ◆ Patterns
- ◆ Cause and effect

**TABLE 3.5** Asking meaningful questions: Life Sciences

| *Asking meaningful questions: Life Sciences* | |
| --- | --- |
| Remember: identify, name, repeat, recall | What is …? |
| Understand: describe, discuss, explain, summarize | What happens if …? |
| Apply: explain why, dramatize, identify with/relate to | Why did or does …? |
| Analyze: recognize change, experiment, infer, compare, contrast | Describe what you observed … |
| Evaluate: express opinion, judge, defend/criticize | What do you think about …? |
| Create: make, construct, design, author | What are your ideas about …? |

See Table 3.5 for a list of meaningful questions about life sciences. See Table 3.6 for a collection of activities appropriate for ESS.

# Science Lesson Plan

### Earth's Systems: Water: The Coast

Any topic from this chapter can be used in place of "The Coast." Water is a large domain for investigation, as you have seen in this chapter. Find an area that is relevant to your teaching situation, interests of your students, and access to community support in the way of experts, resources, or ability to observe a body of water first-hand.

This lesson plan can be taught over a period of days, using the same format, by breaking the activities up as appropriate for your students. First and foremost, find out what your children already know about the topic you will be exploring. This particular lesson focuses on the coast, a place where the land and the ocean meet.

"The Coast" lesson can be simplified, expanded, or modified in a way which works for you, your time, and space, and your students (who may or may not live near a coast). This lesson is about the characteristics of the coast which is a broad focus. Change or adjust as needed for your own purposes. The

**TABLE 3.6** Earth and Space Science activities

| Science | Activities and creative arts |
|---|---|
| Earth's place in the universe | Observe the cycle of day and night |
| | Record information on sunrise/sunset |
| | Observe seasons and changes occurring in our habits (cooler or warmer weather with change in clothing and activities) plants' and animals' behavior in response to seasonal change (spring – birds nesting, leaves emerging, fall/winter – leaves falling, gardens being put to bed) |
| | Night sky: Notice stars and planets from home with support and engagement of family |
| | Create a journal of changes |
| | Relate to the creative Arts: Poetry of day/night: "Taking Turns" by Norma Farber – class discussion about her poem |
| | Stories about night/daytime. Many myths and legends are about the night/day and seasons with origin stories. Share them with the children after a class discussion and observation on cycles – seasons, night/daytime |
| *Earth's Systems* | |
| Rocks | Rich area for exploration, experimentation, observation, hands-on engagement. |
| | Focus on observing characteristics of different rocks while noting where they were found/located |
| | Create collections/sets of rocks sorting, grouping, and arranging using different categories and rules |
| | Example: Location (where found), color, shape, size, feel, type (if it is appropriate to classify according to type – our explorations focus on exploring and investigation) |
| | Sand: location, type, feel, color |
| | Provide magnifying glasses to examine rocks and sand |
| | Sorting bins for categories of rocks and sand |
| | Mural/painting of site where rocks were collected |
| | Sculpture with rocks |
| | Record activities, explorations outside with photos or video to share later with class and families |
| Water: Land and Ocean | Large topic – focus on a specific body of water to investigate |
| | • Ocean |
| | • Lakes |
| | • Ponds |
| | • Rivers |
| | • Coastal waters |

**TABLE 3.6** (*Continued*)

| Science | Activities and creative arts |
|---|---|
| | • Wetlands |
| | • Saltwater and freshwater marshes |
| | Focus on topics of interest and relevancy to your students |
| | Explore water – a water table in the classroom with fresh, then maybe salt, brackish water – hands-on, record children's thoughts, reactions, and feelings |
| | Relate to the creative arts: murals, painting with water and color |
| | Books, poems, songs, music about water |
| | Relate to the creative arts: Movement – fluid and sustained movement – large movements like waves or small actions, like a trickle of water |
| Weather and Climate | Discussion on weather – write down children's responses and thoughts |
| | Activate prior knowledge |
| | Folklore, mythology, legends, and creator myths about weather |
| | Many poems, songs, and stories focus on weather |
| | Relate to the creative arts: seasons, types of weather |
| | Chart favorite season/weather |
| | Relate to the creative arts |
| | Music: reproduce sounds of weather – rain, wind, snow, storms |
| | Different settings/environments have different weather sounds associated with them – living by the ocean or body of water, the sounds will be specific to that setting and environment |
| | Movement/dance: respond to the sounds of weather or create weather-like movements |
| | Drama: lots of stories about weather good for sharing as a presentation |
| | Photos/video: record weather events and share for discussion or comparison |
| *Earth and Human Activity* | |
| Human Impact on Earth Systems | Focus on how humans use and interact with our environment daily and over time. Ties back with NAAEE's Key Aspects on knowing our relationship to nature and our environment in which we live. |
| | Discuss and record thoughts on our relationship to our setting |

(*Continued*)

**TABLE 3.6** (*Continued*)

| Science | Activities and creative arts |
|---|---|
| | Define "setting" before discussion |
| | We use space in our environment for our homes – urban, suburban, and rural |
| | Wood for homes, furniture, toys, books, newspapers, packaging, and wrappings, for example |
| | Gardens for food |
| | Fields for cattle and other farm animals |
| | Fields for growing crops |
| | Relate to the creative arts: |
| | Visual arts: painting, murals, textiles (cotton – plant, wool from sheep, alpacas, rabbits, and goats) |
| | Stories about our use of the Earth |
| | Songs, poems, and music |
| | Dance/movement |
| Natural Resources | Discuss and define natural resources: activate prior knowledge |
| | Chart responses and share thoughts |
| | Spend a good amount of time discussing natural resources – it is a big topic and a lot of information which depends on locations, settings, and environments |
| | Emphasis is on "natural" resources |
| | Include families and locate local experts and those who depend on natural resources for work – farmers, fishermen, loggers, mill workers (wood products, textiles), tourist industry, sports (skiing, snowmobiling, hunting, recreation: boating, camping, hiking) |
| | The connections go all the way to our clothing, foods, homes, and cars/transportation, entertainment, travel, school, where we live and how we live |
| | Relate to the creative arts: |
| | Visual arts: Paint, draw, sculpt scenes or objects representative of this topic as it relates to your children and the community |
| | Drama: Share a story focusing on natural resources and how the characters need/use them |
| | Photo/film: Record, create, share images of natural resources within the local environment–classify and sort the different kinds |

exploration can extend for as long or as short a time depending on your classroom curriculum, schedule and student interest. This is in part a template to be personalized. Have fun!

♦ *Age range*: 3–8 years old: Preschool/Early Elementary.
♦ *Instructional objective*: Introduce the children to the concept of the "coast" and explore its characteristics.
♦ *Learning target*: Explore the idea of "coast," what does that mean to each child and what are their experiences, if any, of being on a coast? Investigate the various attributes of the applicable ocean and the land which meets it.

Now introduce the topic:

♦ Activate their prior knowledge: whole-class discussion with chart paper or whiteboard to record and save their ideas.
♦ Open-ended questions: e.g. *"What is the coast? Can you tell me more?" "What have you noticed about the coast if you have been there?"*
♦ Once you sense the children are ready to move on or have exhausted the list, do a quick review with a bit of adding or re-stating if a contribution was not clear.
♦ Share posters or digital images of the specific coast you are studying.
♦ Books: There are many books about the coast and coastal waters. I have included some here focusing on the coast of Maine.
  ♦ *On Grandpa's Beach in Maine: A Little Story About A Big Rock* by Pamela Baxter
  ♦ *Lobsterman* by Dahlov Ipcar
  ♦ *The Journey of the Little Red Boat* by George Smith
  ♦ *My Maine* by Suzanne Buzby Hersey
  ♦ *A Seaside Alphabet* by Donna Grassby.

Choose a story to share with the class at this time, asking them to be on the lookout for some of the characteristics they listed for "the coast." This might be a stopping place or an opportunity to do an art activity.

- ◆ Creative art activity: Visual arts – using different mediums on different surfaces, provide children with the time and space to explore and represent the coast and coastal waters.
  - ◆ Having at hand some of the items found at the coast – rocks, sand, seaweed, shells – is useful.
  - ◆ Children can incorporate these items into their art projects which could be painting, sculpture, or a collage.

Music, singing, dance, and writing are all vehicles for further exploration and expression of the coast.

- ◆ Assessment:
  - ◆ Were all the children engaged?
  - ◆ Were all the children able to participate?
- ◆ Developmentally Appropriate Practice:
  - ◆ *Families*: Reach out to families prior to the lessons to see if there are any experts or resources. Also let the families know what their child will be doing in class for a few days.
  - ◆ *Intentional teaching*: Ask thoughtful, child-centric, open-ended questions, support all learners where they are developmentally.

## Extension

### Deeper Dive into "the Coast"
Choose a specific area of investigation. The area you choose can focus on any specific attribute or characteristic of the coast which is relevant and interesting to your learners. Use posters, videos, books, and poetry to extend children's experience with the coast. Invite experts into the classroom to share their expertise. If possible or feasible, take a field trip to the nearest coast for a first-hand, hands-on exploration.

- Classroom hands-on activity to explore sand, rocks, salt water, shells, seaweed, and other objects found at the coast.
- Count, compare, sort, and identify attributes of objects.
- Characteristics of the coast. What does the environment look like? Can different types of coastal environments be classified into zones (e.g. tidal, dunes, etc.)?
  - Sand
  - Rocks
  - Mud
  - Gravel
  - Sand dunes
  - Water
  - Does the tree line meet the water?
  - Dune grass

Who lives there?

- Animals
- Humans
- Plants
  - Seaweed
  - Dune grass
  - Pines
  - Grasses
- Birds in spring
- Clams, mussels, barnacles, razor clams, quahogs, sand dollars.

What happens where the water meets the land?

- People
  - Swim
  - Go boating
  - Wading
  - Go walking
  - Build sandcastles and other structures
  - Explore.

- ◆ Animals
  - ◆ Build nests
  - ◆ Forage for food
  - ◆ Shelter.
- ◆ Plants

What happens when the water meets the land?

- ◆ Storms
- ◆ Tides
- ◆ Debris
- ◆ Erosion
- ◆ Shifting sands and coastlines.

Now conclude by asking:

- ◆ Assessment:
  - ◆ Were all the children engaged?
  - ◆ Were all the children able to participate?
- ◆ Developmentally Appropriate Practice:
  - ◆ *Families*: Reach out to families prior to the lessons to see if there are any experts or resources. Also let the families know what their child will be doing in class for a few days.
  - ◆ *Intentional teaching*: Ask thoughtful, child-centric, open-ended questions, support all learners where they are developmentally.

## Project Ideas

- ◆ Puppet theater: Choose a focus from your study of the coast and have the children tell a story using puppets. Make finger puppets, sock puppets, silhouette puppets, or cutout puppets.
- ◆ Mural: Focus on a specific topic of interest to your students and create a mural. The outline should be penciled in before the children work on it. Include in the composition characteristics and objects the children determine when discussing ideas.

This project aspect should be flexible, reflecting the children's interests, abilities, and developmental skills.

## Conclusion

- ◆ Assessment:
    - ◆ Were all the children engaged?
    - ◆ Were they able to demonstrate understanding of "coastal" systems?
    - ◆ Were all the children able to participate?
- ◆ Developmentally Appropriate Practice:
    - ◆ *Families*: Reach out to families prior to the lessons to see if there are any experts or resources. Also let the families know what their child will be doing in class for a few days.
    - ◆ *Intentional teaching*: Ask thoughtful, child-centric, open-ended questions, support all learners where they are developmentally.

See Table 3.7 for skill sets and Developmentally Appropriate Practice.

See Table 3.8 for a list of the creative arts and suggestions for integrating into the Sciences.

## Notes

1   Astrophysics is a branch of science which uses the laws of physics and chemistry to understand the universe and our place in it; Geophysics: explores the physical processes and physical properties of the Earth; Geochemistry represents the science of the chemical properties of the Earth, its rocks, and minerals; and Geobiology explores the interactions between the physical Earth and the biosphere (parts of the Earth where life exists).

2   Atmosphere: the layers of gases surrounding the Earth; hydrosphere: total amount of water on the Earth, including surface, underground, and in the air; geosphere: all the rocks and minerals that make up Earth: biosphere: parts of the Earth where life exists.

**TABLE 3.7** Science Grid of skill sets and DAP

| Stage | Skill Sets | Learning expectations | Scaffolding strategies | Access prior knowledge | Asking meaningful/probing questions (NAEYC, 2017) | DAP (NAEYC, 2020) |
|---|---|---|---|---|---|---|
| Toddler: 16–36 months | Dependence on adults<br><br>Learning to speak<br><br>Coordinate sensations and physical activities<br><br>Think with symbols<br><br>Imitate and learn from others | Engagement<br><br>Interest<br><br>Exploration<br><br>Asking questions | Verbal encouragement<br><br>Demonstration<br><br>Physical support<br><br>Patience | Observation<br><br>Asking probing questions<br><br>Being an attentive listener | *Levels of questioning and expected response or behavior from the child*<br><br>Remember: identify, name, count, repeat, recall<br><br>Understand: describe, discuss, explain, summarize<br><br>Apply: Explain why, dramatize, identify with/relate to<br><br>Analyze: recognize change, experiment, infer, compare, contrast<br><br>Evaluate: express opinion, judge, defend/criticize<br><br>Create: make, construct, design, author | Relationship with primary caregiver established as warm and welcoming<br><br>Learn toddler's ways and habits from observation and interactions<br><br>Acceptance and adjust to toddler's ways and preferences<br><br>Responsive to toddler's needs<br><br>Environment appropriate for the toddler with different spaces (quiet, play, small group, individual), with toys to manipulate and explore<br><br>Indoor and outdoor spaces |

| Preschool: 3–5 years | Curriculum and activities enhances development – physical (small and gross motor), social and emotional, and cognitive (language: listening, speaking, and understanding)

Reading and writing (attendant skills) | Curiosity about the world around them

Engagement with exploration, experimentation, and observation

Engagement with science activities – question asking, providing theories | Asking questions

Observation

Verbal encouragement

Demonstration

Physical support

Patience

Adult or peer demonstrates skill set | Observation

Asking probing questions

Being an attentive listener

Use of a KWL chart or something similar | *Levels of questioning and expected response or behavior from the child*

Remember: identify, name, count, repeat, recall

Understand: describe, discuss, explain, summarize

Apply: Explain why, dramatize, identify with/relate to

Analyze: recognize change, experiment, infer, compare, contrast

Evaluate: express opinion, judge, defend/criticize

Create: make, construct, design, author | Foster positive relationships

Build classroom community

Safe, healthy environment promotes independence and exploration w/clear boundaries

Spaces promote variety of learning opportunities: small group, large group, individual

Different areas arranged to promote different learning styles |

(Continued)

**TABLE 3.7** (Continued)

| Stage | Skill Sets | Learning expectations | Scaffolding strategies | Access prior knowledge | Asking meaningful/ probing questions (NAEYC, 2017) | DAP (NAEYC, 2020) |
|---|---|---|---|---|---|---|
| Kindergarten: 5–6 years | Curriculum and activities enhances development – physical (small and gross motor), social and emotional, and cognitive (language: listening, speaking, and understanding)<br><br>Reading and writing (attendant skills)<br><br>Develop vocabulary – language of science | Curiosity about the world around them<br><br>Engagement with exploration, experimentation, and observation<br><br>Provide materials for exploration, manipulation, and experimentation<br><br>Engagement with science activities – question asking, providing theories | Asking questions<br><br>Observation<br><br>Verbal encouragement<br><br>Demonstration<br><br>Physical support<br><br>Patience<br><br>Adult or peer demonstrates skill set | Observation<br><br>Asking probing questions<br><br>Being an attentive listener<br><br>Use of a KWL chart or something similar | Levels of questioning and expected response or behavior from the child<br><br>Remember: identify, name, count, repeat, recall<br><br>Understand: describe, discuss, explain, summarize<br><br>Apply: Explain why, dramatize, identify with/relate to<br><br>Analyze: recognize change, experiment, infer, compare, contrast<br><br>Evaluate: express opinion, judge, defend/criticize<br><br>Create: make, construct, design, author | Foster positive relationships<br><br>Build classroom community<br><br>Learning environment promotes exploration, initiative, positive peer interaction, and cognitive growth<br><br>Spaces promote variety of learning opportunities: small group, large group, individual<br><br>Different areas arranged to promote different learning styles |

| Primary Grades: 6–8 years | | | | Observation | Levels of questioning and expected response or behavior from the child | |
|---|---|---|---|---|---|---|
| | Curriculum and activities enhances development – physical (small and gross motor), social and emotional, and cognitive (language: listening, speaking, and understanding, word and print knowledge, phonemic awareness) Reading and writing (attendant skills) Develop vocabulary – language of science | Plan and conduct investigations Analyze data Make observations and communicate outcomes of observations Use tools and materials to design and build models Develop an argument supported by evidence to support a theory Ask questions to obtain information Communicate outcomes of observations and experiments to others | Asking questions Observation Verbal encouragement Demonstration Physical support Patience Adult or peer demonstrates skill set | Asking probing questions Being an attentive listener Use of a KWL chart or something similar | Remember: identify, name, count, repeat, recall Understand: describe, discuss, explain, summarize Apply: Explain why, dramatize, identify with/relate to Analyze: recognize change, experiment, infer, compare, contrast Evaluate: express opinion, judge, defend/criticize Create: make, construct, design, author | Teachers know each child and create a community of learners who support each other Children work collaboratively Teachers respect children's opinions and ways of thinking Classroom environment enhances learning through thoughtful arrangement of furniture and knowledge of each child's learning style Learning environment supports exploration, initiative, positive peer interaction and cognitive growth |

**TABLE 3.8** Arts Grid for the sciences

| Stage | Theater/drama/puppets | Music | Singing | Movement/dance | Visual arts | Creative writing | Photography/Film |
|---|---|---|---|---|---|---|---|
| Toddler: 13–36 months | Simple play – games<br>Finger play<br>Puppet play<br>Poetry / poems | Simple percussion<br>Clapping<br>Patting legs or other body parts or floor<br>Themed music | Nursery rhymes<br>Songs that repeat and build<br>Dynamics of song – high/low, loud, soft, quick/slow | Simple movement actions<br>Different types of movement<br>Different dynamics<br>Fast, slow | Exploring shapes and lines<br>Exploring marks on paper<br>Exploring color<br>Exploring types of paint application – finger paints, or painting with other items | Placing marks on paper representative or symbolic for concepts, concrete ideas, or objects<br>Simple stories dictated to an adult or simple stories with symbolic marks representative of ideas or objects<br>Poetry / poems | Record either with a camera or video events, objects of meaning, or places<br>Photograph projects for sharing |
| Preschool: 3–5 years | Simple play – games<br>Finger play<br>Puppet play<br>Act out a short story<br>Poetry / poems | Simple percussion<br>Clapping<br>Patting legs or other body parts or floor<br>Themed music | Nursery rhymes<br>Songs that repeat and build<br>Dynamics of song – high/low, loud, soft, quick/slow | Simple movement actions<br>Different types of movement<br>Different dynamics<br>Fast, slow<br>Move to sound or music<br>Circle dance – follow directions<br>(move in, move out, walk slowly holding hands in a circle, and so on) | Exploring shapes and lines<br>Exploring marks on paper<br>Exploring color<br>Creating new colors<br>Exploring types of paint application – finger paints, or painting with other items<br>Share art of professionals and illustrators | Placing marks on paper representative or symbolic for concepts, concrete ideas, or objects<br>Simple stories dictated to an adult or simple stories with symbolic marks representative of ideas or objects<br>Continue to develop writing skills and story-making<br>Poetry / poems | Record either with a camera or video events, objects of meaning, or places<br>Photograph projects for sharing<br>Child begins to use camera and video |

| Kindergarten: 5–6 years | | | | | | | |
|---|---|---|---|---|---|---|---|
| Simple play – games | Simple percussion | Nursery rhymes | Simple movement actions | Exploring shapes and lines | Placing marks on paper representative or symbolic for concepts, concrete ideas, or objects | Record either with a camera or video events, objects of meaning, or places |
| Finger play | Clapping | Songs that repeat and build | Different types of movement | Exploring marks on paper | | Photograph projects for sharing |
| Puppet play | Patting legs or other body parts or floor | Dynamics of song – high/low, loud, soft, quick/slow | Different dynamics | Exploring color | Simple stories dictated to an adult or simple stories with symbolic marks representative of ideas or objects | Child begins to use camera and video |
| Act out a short story | Themed music | Introduce more complex songs with refrains, chorus, and different verses | Fast, slow | Creating new colors | | Film a play, dance, music performance, an art exhibit |
| Take a favorite story and devise a play | Introduce instruments for playing tambourine, sticks, drums | Imitate, extend songs | Move to different sounds or different types of music | Exploring types of paint application – finger paints, or painting with other items | Continue to develop writing skills and story-making | |
| Begin to incorporate the other arts into drama | Create simple clapping patterns or rhythms for children to copy and add on to | Act out songs | Circle dance – follow directions | Share art of professionals | Create stories with a beginning, middle, and end | |
| Act out songs | Find objects in the room or outside to use for percussion or rhythm | Songs with repetition for acting | (move in, move out, walk slowly holding hands in a circle, and so on) | Art exploration with different mediums, different forms of expression, different materials, different goals | Text with illustrations | |
| Songs with repetition for acting | | | Begin to develop more complex movement actions | | Share writings | |
| Poetry/ poems | | | Fast, slow, high, low, twist, straight, curvy, with a partner, solo, in a group, move in, move out and so on | | Poetry – create, share and respond | |
| | | | Teach folk dances or improvise a dance to a well-known and liked song | | | |

(Continued)

TABLE 3.8 (Continued)

| Stage | Theater/ drama/puppets | Music | Singing | Movement/dance | Visual arts | Creative writing | Photography/Film |
|---|---|---|---|---|---|---|---|
| Primary Grades: 6–8 years | Puppet play Act out a short story Take a favorite story and devise a play Begin to incorporate the other arts into drama Act out songs Songs with repetition for acting Participate in a play Choose a theme and write a play centered around the chosen theme | Simple percussion Clapping Patting legs or other body parts or floor Themed music Introduce instruments for playing tambourine, sticks, drums Create simple clapping patterns or rhythms for children to copy and add on to Find objects in the room or outside to use for percussion or rhythm | Nursery rhymes Songs that repeat and build Dynamics of song – high/ low, loud, soft, quick/ slow Introduce more complex songs with refrains, chorus, and different verses Imitate, extend songs Act out songs Songs with repetition for acting | Simple movement actions Different types of movement Different dynamics Fast, slow Move to different sounds or different types of music Circle dance – follow directions (move in, move out, walk slowly holding hands in a circle, and so on) Begin to develop more complex movement actions Fast, slow, high, low, twist, straight, curvy, with a partner, solo, in a group, move in, move out and so on | Art exploration with different mediums, different forms of expression, different materials, different goals Continue to explore art from different perspectives, mediums, and themes | Create stories with a beginning, middle, and end Text with illustrations Share writings Poetry – read, create, share Stories reflect themes with complexity of action, characters, and message | Record either with a camera or video events, objects of meaning, or places Photograph projects for sharing Child begins to use camera and video Film a play, dance, music performance, an art exhibit Continue to explore ways of using film and video |

| | | | |
|---|---|---|---|
| Choose a theme and improvise a story | Continue to develop complexity in music and use of instruments with the addition of voice and movement | Continue to develop complexity in song format and style<br><br>Layer onto music and drama | Teach folk dances or improvise a dance to a well-known and liked song<br><br>Continue to develop complexity in movement and dance<br><br>Add movement and dance to drama, music, and song |

# 4

# The Case for Technology in Early Childhood Education

## Introduction

As early childhood educators, we tend to view the use of digital devices and screen time for young children with doubt and skepticism. Too much screen time (regardless of the screen being used) can be detrimental in many ways. We value community, interactive engagement, and play, all of which can be negatively impacted through too much solitary screen-viewing! Yet, there is much to recommend the thoughtful and informed integration of different technologies into the early childhood experience in the classroom. One of integrational technology's early proponents was Fred Rogers (*Mr. Rogers' Neighborhood*) who valued above all else the uniqueness of each child and of finding ways to engage that uniqueness.

The rich potential of technology can improve and enrich early childhood education programs, benefiting *all* children as long as educators are knowledgeable about developmental practices and how to effectively *integrate* technology and interactive media into the curriculum (NAEYC and Fred Rogers Center, 2012).

In this chapter I share strategies, appropriate develop-mental approaches, types of technology approved by national organizations, and methods of implementation to support and

DOI: 10.4324/9781003395614-4

enhance the early childhood curriculum. Technology has become an integral component of our lives in many ways. Understanding the ways technology can be harnessed to enhance and deepen learning is our job as thoughtful educators. Use the Technology Grid (Table 4.3) at the end of the chapter for guidance with appropriate developmental activities and expectations. The Arts Grid (Table 4.4) at the end of the chapter provides activity ideas young children will enjoy, supporting technology experiences.

A short summary is given below of the "Principles to Guide the Appropriate Use of Technology and Interactive Media as Tools in Early Childhood Programs Serving Children from Birth through Age 8" (NAEYC and Fred Rogers Center, 2012).

## Guidelines for Interactive Media and Technology

◆ Interactive media vs non-interactive media:
  ◆ Eliminate non-interactive media for young children.
◆ No screen time for infants and toddlers:
  ◆ This guideline has been given a caveat: for families living a-distance from each other, they can connect via (and benefit from) screen time with young children or grandchildren. This can be a valuable experience for all involved. Being able to connect via digital videoing with my new grandchild far away has been profoundly rewarding.
◆ Limited screen time for young children:
  ◆ Defining screen time: time spent in front of a digital device with a screen.
◆ Monitor the amount of time spent with screen-oriented media.
◆ Pay attention to how children spend time with digital media.
◆ Issues of equity and access are important. Access and equity for all are key elements of planning for the integration of technology into the classroom.

Developmentally appropriate practice (DAP) should guide your decisions about when and what to integrate into the classroom experiences. As the teacher, it is your professional judgment that is required to determine the appropriateness of technology to be used. Appropriateness is determined on an individual, cultural, and linguistic level. What each child needs and is interested in directs the type of media used. The context of each child's social and cultural experience contributes to the larger picture of media appropriateness. The language of each child directs access to the type of digital media. Interactive media has its own language and ways of communicating information. Young children can quickly adapt to this with support and exposure that is appropriate to the child. Age, developmental level, needs, interests, linguistic background, and abilities direct use of technology (as it would for any curriculum).

As you plan for technology to become part of your curriculum and the children's regular activities, give careful consideration to the type of technology and to the available programs using that technology type. Digital experiences with young children should be creative so children's imaginations are engaged. The experiences should be playful, which appeals to the learner. Make sure an element of exploration is present – how do things work?, what does this mean?, how can we get from here to there?

Assistive technology was described in *The Individuals with Disabilities Education Improvement Act* of 2004 (IDEA; www.idea.ed.gov) as "any item, piece of equipment, or product system, whether acquired commercially, modified, or customized, that is used to increase, maintain, or improve functional capabilities of individuals with disabilities." Assistive technology can be a tool used in a variety of ways to provide support for cognitive processing. For dual-language learners, technology can provide access to the family's home language and culture while supporting the learning of the English language.

Children as young as 2 to 3 years-old are able to understand and formulate abstract ideas. Technology can help children bridge the world between concrete and abstract notions, especially in math. Multiple representations of ideas on the computer or other screen-based technology can help children make connections between the abstract and the concrete. Seeing something on the screen can be as significant to the child as holding or manipulating an item or items. For example, the concreteness of a specific number – say, three – reinforced through seeing three items presented on the screen carries meaning much in the same way as holding three items in the hand does.

Embed technology in a rich educational environment where you as the teacher control the technology and your children's use of it. The technology used should ideally represent only a relatively small part of the children's day and educational experience. Your presence is important to the child's learning and positive experience. Your students are more likely to learn if you, as an interested adult, are present or nearby. Activities with technology should be open-ended, developmentally appropriate, and reflect curriculum objectives. Start where you are most comfortable and where your own strengths lie.

The following three guiding principles, which were developed by the Fred Roger's Center for Early Learning and Children's Media at Saint Vincent College (2012) and titled "A Framework for Quality in Digital Media for Young Children: Considerations for Parents, Educators, and Media Creators," provide direction for you in considering technology in your classroom.

### Principle 1: Quality Digital Media Should Safeguard the Health, Well-Being, and Overall Development of Young Children

As noted in Chapter 1, the nurturing and receptive interactions between the child and caregiver foster healthy development in the child. Creative play, social interactions involving language, reading, conversation, questions asked, paying close attention to the child's state of being, all contribute to healthy cognitive, social, emotional, physical, and linguistic development. Digital media should never detract from or diminish these important developmental experiences.

### Principle 2: Quality in Digital Media for Young Children Should Take into Account the Child, the Content, and the Context of Use

When evaluating digital media for your learners, consider who you are choosing for, what is the content of the digital media, and how it will be used. Ask these questions: does this digital device, tool, or technology meet the needs of each child, their interests, and developmental stage? How does the content of this device or tool help each child in his or her developmental journey? Does it engage the child with language, allow the child to explore, play, or imagine?

Finally, consider the context of use. Will the particular digital device support the child's growth and development? Any digital tool or device should enhance play and the interaction between the child and another, whether it is parent, caregiver, or playmate.

### Principle 3: Determinations of Quality

Principle 3 in full is:

> Determinations of quality should be grounded in an evidence base that can be used by parents, educators, policymakers, and others to make decisions about the selection and use of particular digital media products, and by media creators to improve and develop new products in response to consumer expectations of quality.

Unfortunately the scope of available research and literature on the effects of screen time on young children probably does not meet the needs of educators and parents regarding the outcomes of multiple digital devices, each featuring a screen. New research is required to further investigate the impacts of screen time, whether in formal or informal learning situations. Parents, caregivers, and educators of young children need information in order to make informed and appropriate choices regarding digital media and devices. In the absence of such documented information, or in lieu of a school-based technology policy that should or must be followed, educators should individually strive to obtain the most up-to-date information available regarding the appropriate use(s) of technology for the age range(s) they instruct.

### Questions for Educators to Ask and to Guide Them When Considering Technology for the Early Childhood Classroom

In addition to the Principles from the Fred Roger's Institute, the Early Childhood Educational Technology Evaluation Toolkit (McManis & Parks, 2011) can help guide and inform digital media choices. Listed are the six primary areas for consideration when researching digital media and technology for your young learners:

- ◆ Educational value
- ◆ Appropriateness
- ◆ Child-friendliness
- ◆ Enjoyable/engaging
- ◆ Progress monitoring/assessment
- ◆ Individualizing features.

## Technology-Enhanced Adult-Child Relationships

Many devices, such as those enabling shared screen experiences, texting, and the use of publishing or social media-type apps should be carefully evaluated before using them in a classroom setting. I know I have many conversations with my grandchildren, who live a distance from me, through texting. I learn much about their activities, feelings, and thoughts. Opportunities for turn-taking and sharing are embedded in certain digital experiences. There are many studies demonstrating that more learning occurs when experiences are social rather than happening in isolation. The term *social contingency* translates into a response which is immediate and accurate in content when individuals are communicating through social media. Responses such as these generate richer and deeper social exchanges. One other socially shared experience to note involves screen-sharing opportunities which have been created by the teacher for co-viewing and adjacent viewing.

## Additional Thoughts on Using Technology Tools

1. Record children's voices as they tell a story and play it back to them.
2. Make a book of what happened during the day, using pictures from a smartphone or digital camera.
3. Use old inactive cell phones to promote conversations and engage in imaginary play (remove the battery first!).
4. Think of digital and other electronic media as you would a book. Be present with the child and play with the technology together.

5. Children are engaged in new technologies because they are often exciting and they see the adults in their lives using them. Promote their curiosity, pick high-quality and age-appropriate content, and be thoughtful about how technology fits into your learning goals!

6. As a parent, next time you ask your child how their day was, use imaginary phones (such as an old cell phone, a banana, or even just your fingers).

7. When you go on a walk or trip, take pictures of what you see. Print the pictures to make a story book. Even if a child cannot read yet, you can ask him or her to tell you what is happening in the pictures. Or, flip through the pictures on the device and ask the child to describe what's happening in the pictures.

8. When we introduce children to technology and innovation, we are inviting them to dream, imagine, and create.

Table 4.1 illustrates some relevant questions that can be asked of learners to help evaluate their current or ongoing experience with the technology tool.

Table 4.2 covers some technology activities you can explore with your class.

**TABLE 4.1** Asking meaningful questions: technology

| Actions | Questions |
| --- | --- |
| Remember: identify, name, repeat, recall | What is the name of this game you are playing on your computer (laptop, iPad, etc.)? |
| Understand: describe, discuss, explain, summarize | What can you tell me about this game you are playing? |
| Apply: explain why, dramatize, identify with/relate to | How would you explain your choice of action? |
| Analyze: recognize change, experiment, infer, compare, contrast | Explain what happened after you used the mouse (computer mouse)? |
| Evaluate: express opinion, judge, defend/criticize | Tell me what you enjoy about this activity or game and why |
| Create: make, construct, design, author | Create a new digital game using the coding instructions. |

**TABLE 4.2** Technology activities

| Technology (some examples) | Activities and creative arts |
|---|---|
| Bee-Bot® programmable robot: It can be programmed to move forward, or sideways, and backwards. | Program the robot to accomplish a task on a game, number, or letter board |
| Interactive whiteboard | Program the interactive whiteboard to accomplish certain tasks which children will be able to accomplish independently through interacting with the whiteboard |
| 3Doodler start + | Appropriate for older children (6+) 3D pens for young children. Create 3D shapes and designs. |
| Augmented reality: ©Blippar App | Combine art portraits with recorded interviews of individuals represented in the portraits |
| Makerspace | A designated space in the classroom for experimentation, exploration, testing, and refining ideas. Incorporate appropriate technology and digital devices to enhance the experience. |
| iPad/Touch Tablet | Interactive activities where the learner is able to touch screen to manipulate objects |
| Cubetto | Screenless coding – children experience spatial orientation and exploration as they envision the directions they want Cubetto to travel and then code for |
| Digital frames | Sharing experiences from the day with family or others. Upload images or videos to the digital frame and then watch them as they are displayed. |
| Digital cameras | Capturing images, events, objects, and recordings to use in classroom projects, school-home communication, and the school-wide community. Images can be uploaded to websites, cell phones, and digital frames. They can be printed up for sharing on a bulletin board or showcased on posters. |
| Interactive smart whiteboard | Classroom engagement, manipulation, and collaboration through use of a whiteboard in the classroom using touchscreen technology Touchscreen technology provides interactive opportunities for young student |

## Technology Lesson Plan

### Bee-Bot® Programmable Robot

Bee-Bot is a small robot in the form of a bee which can be programmed or coded to move in specific directions over specific distances through coding (Figure 4.1). Coding is a set of instructions for a computer. In addition to coding as part of the learning, spatial sense, spatial orientation, planning Bee-Bot's moves, and executing the plan for Bee-Bot are also key skills in this lesson.

Change or adjust the lesson as needed for your own purposes. The exploration can extend for as long or as short a time, depending on your classroom curriculum, schedule, and student interest. This is in part a template to be personalized. Have fun!

♦ *Age range*: 3 or 4–8 years old: Preschool/early elementary.
♦ *Instructional objective*: Introduce the children to the concept of coding.
♦ *Learning target*: Explore the concept of coding through programming Bee-Bot. Play, experiment, and test to determine if their coding or programming works. Explore the notion of spatial orientation, movement, directionality, distance, planning, and teamwork with Bee-Bot and coding.

FIGURE 4.1 Bee-Bot.

*Introduction*

- ◆ Activate their prior knowledge: Whole class discussion with chart paper or whiteboard to record and save their ideas. Most children even at the young age of 3 or 4 will have had exposure to phones, laptops, tablets, and screens in general. Robots will be familiar to some children.
- ◆ Open-ended questions: *"What can you tell me about robots?," "How do robots move about?," "Can robots read directions about where to move?" "Tell me more." "What do know about coding?" "Tell me more."*
- ◆ Once you sense the children are ready to move on or have exhausted the list, do a quick review with a bit of adding or re-stating if a contribution was not clear.
- ◆ Introduce Bee-Bot. Let the children see the robot and explain its different parts. The controls are on top: forward, backward, right turn, left turn, and start/clear. Underneath are wheels.
- ◆ Ask the children what they notice. Take some time to let them look over Bee-Bot and record their observations.
- ◆ Ask: *"How does Bee-Bot move?"*
  - ◆ Note responses – record if appropriate.
  - ◆ Ask what they notice on top of Bee-Bot. The controls are located on top.
  - ◆ Lead the children into offering suggestions about how to get Bee-Bot to move and then test out their ideas.

Bee-Bot has to be programmed to move in any direction. Each push of a button allows it to move a designated space. When Bee-Bot has moved the designated space, it beeps and stops. One forward command moves it one Bee-Bot space forward. A turn command turns the Bee-Bot, it does not move it ahead. That must be programmed. Afterwards, do the following:

- ◆ Take time to explore with the children and experiment with the robot.
- ◆ Assessment:

- ◆ Were all the children engaged?
- ◆ Were all the children able to participate?
- ◆ Developmentally Appropriate Practice:
    - ◆ *Families*: Reach out to families prior to the lessons to see if there are any experts or resources. Also let the families know what their child will be doing in class for a few days.
    - ◆ *Intentional teaching*: Ask thoughtful, child-centric, open-ended questions, support all learners where they are developmentally.

## Extension #1

- ◆ *Learning target*: Extend programming and apply to an activity:
    - ◆ Have a large floor grid ready with squares about the size of Bee-Bot. The grid is where the robot will move around according to the directions or programming the class has given it.
- ◆ *Computer language/coding*: the language Bee-Bot understands is made up of arrows as commands. It does not understand English, Spanish, French, or any language which might be spoken in your class.
    - ◆ Program the robot to move on the floor grid according to the directions of the students.
    - ◆ Test – outcome: did it work?
    - ◆ Revisit or reprogram to continue.

## Additional Extensions

- ◆ Revisit the previous lesson. Ask thoughtful and probing questions about what happened and what they learned.
    - ◆ Note responses. Their feedback informs your next lesson or activity.
- ◆ If appropriate, introduce a large floor grid with letters of the alphabet with one letter in each square. The children program the robot to spell out their names.
- ◆ With blocks, build a roadway with a turn or so and program the robot to navigate the road correctly, including distance to the end.

♦ Assessment:
♦ Were all the children engaged?
♦ Were all the children able to participate?
♦ Developmentally Appropriate Practice:
  ♦ *Families*: Reach out to families prior to the lessons to see if there are any experts or resources. Also let the families know what their child will be doing in class for a few days.
  ♦ *Intentional teaching*: Ask thoughtful, child-centric, open-ended questions, support all learners where they are developmentally.

## Conclusion

Revisit this lesson. Ask thoughtful and probing questions about what happened and what they learned.

**TABLE 4.3** Technology Grid of skill sets and DAP

| Stage | Skill sets | Learning expectations | Scaffolding strategies | Access prior knowledge | Asking good/meaningful/probing questions (Strasser & Mufson Bresson, 2017) | DAP (NAEYC, 2020) |
|---|---|---|---|---|---|---|
| Toddler: 13–36 months | Dependence on adults<br><br>Learning to speak<br><br>Coordinate sensations and physical activities<br><br>Think with symbols<br><br>Imitate and learn from others (Santrock, 2019) | DAP with Technology (NAEYC, 2020)<br><br>Explore digital materials: shared technology – interactions between child and adult<br><br>Avoid passive screen time<br><br>Technology as an active and engaging tool when appropriate<br><br>Incorporate assistive technology as appropriate for children with special needs and/or developmental delays | Verbal encouragement<br><br>Demonstration<br><br>Physical support<br><br>Patience | Observation<br><br>Asking probing questions<br><br>Being an attentive listener | Levels of questioning and expected response or behavior from the child<br><br>Remember: identify, name, count, repeat, recall<br><br>Understand: describe, discuss, explain, summarize<br><br>Apply: explain why, dramatize, identify with/relate to<br><br>Analyze: recognize change, experiment, infer, compare, contrast<br><br>Evaluate: express opinion, judge, defend/criticize<br><br>Create: make, construct, design, author | Relationship with primary caregiver established as warm and welcoming<br><br>Learn toddler's ways and habits from observation and interactions<br><br>Acceptance and adjust to toddler's ways and preferences<br><br>Responsive to toddler's needs<br><br>Environment appropriate for the toddler with different spaces (quiet, play, small group, individual), with toys to manipulate and explore<br><br>Indoor and outdoor spaces |

| Preschool: 3–5 years | Curriculum and activities enhances development – physical (small and gross motor), social and emotional, and cognitive (language: listening, speaking, and understanding) Reading and writing (attendant skills) | DAP with Technology (NAEYC, 2020) Allow children to freely explore touch screens (with developmentally appropriate interactive media) Provide opportunities for children to explore and feel comfortable using traditional mouse and keyboard computers to use websites or look up answers with a search engine Photograph projects or creations in the classroom Celebrate accomplishments with digital media Incorporate assistive technology as appropriate for children with special needs and/or developmental delays | Asking questions Observation Verbal encouragement Demonstration Physical support Patience Adult or peer demonstrates skill set | Observation Asking probing questions Being an attentive listener Use of a KWL chart or something similar | Levels of questioning and expected response or behavior from the child Remember: identify, name, count, repeat, recall Understand: describe, discuss, explain, summarize Apply: explain why, dramatize, identify with/relate to Analyze: recognize change, experiment, infer, compare, contrast Evaluate: express opinion, judge, defend/criticize Create: make, construct, design, author | Foster positive relationships Build classroom community Safe, healthy environment promotes independence and exploration with clear boundaries Spaces promote variety of learning opportunities: small group, large group, individual Different areas arranged to promote different learning styles |

*(Continued)*

**TABLE 4.3** (*Continued*)

| Stage | Skill sets | Learning expectations | Scaffolding strategies | Access prior knowledge | Asking good/meaningful/ probing questions (Strasser & Mufson Bresson, 2017) | DAP (NAEYC, 2020) |
|---|---|---|---|---|---|---|
| Kindergarten: 5–6 years | Curriculum and activities enhances development – physical (small and gross motor), social and emotional, and cognitive (language: listening, speaking, and understanding) Reading and writing (attendant skills) Develop vocabulary–language of technology | DAP with Technology (NAEYC, 2020) Allow children to freely explore touch screens (with developmentally appropriate interactive media) Provide opportunities for children to explore and feel comfortable using traditional mouse and keyboard computers to use websites or look up answers with a search engine Photograph projects or creations in the classroom Celebrate accomplishments with digital media Incorporate assistive technology as appropriate for children with special needs and/or developmental delays Record children's stories Explore digital storytelling | Asking questions Observation Verbal encouragement Demonstration Physical support Patience Adult or peer demonstrates skill set Digital collaboration and modeling | Observation Asking probing questions Being an attentive listener Use of a KWL chart or something similar | Levels of questioning and expected response or behavior from the child Remember: identify, name, count, repeat, recall Understand: describe, discuss, explain, summarize Apply: explain why, dramatize, identify with/relate to • Analyze: recognize change, experiment, infer, compare, contrast Evaluate: express opinion, judge, defend/ criticize Create: make, construct, design, author | Foster positive relationships Build classroom community Learning environment promotes exploration, initiative, positive peer interaction, and cognitive growth Spaces promote variety of learning opportunities: small group, large group, individual Different areas arranged to promote different learning styles |

| Primary Grades: 6–8 years | Curriculum and activities enhances development – physical (small and gross motor), social and emotional, and cognitive (language: listening, speaking, and understanding, word and print knowledge, phonemic awareness)<br><br>Reading and writing (attendant skills)<br><br>Develop vocabulary–language of technology | Share e-books<br><br>Use digital microscopes<br><br>Video-conferencing software<br><br>Arrange play experiences for children to construct and explore their ideas about how technology works<br><br>Provide access to photographs and experiences children may not otherwise encounter<br><br>DAP with Technology (NAEYC, 2020)<br><br>Allow children to freely explore touch screens (with developmentally appropriate interactive media)<br><br>Provide opportunities for children to explore using traditional mouse and keyboard computers to use websites or look up answers with a search engine<br><br>Photograph projects or creations in the classroom<br><br>Celebrate accomplishments with digital media | Asking questions<br><br>Observation<br><br>Verbal encouragement<br><br>Demonstration<br><br>Physical support<br><br>Patience<br><br>Adult or peer demonstrates skill set | Observation<br><br>Asking probing questions<br><br>Being an attentive listener<br><br>Use of a KWL chart or something similar | Levels of questioning and expected response or behavior from the child<br><br>Remember: identify, name, count, repeat, recall<br><br>Understand: describe, discuss, explain, summarize<br><br>Apply: explain why, dramatize, identify with/relate to<br><br>Analyze: recognize change, experiment, infer, compare, contrast<br><br>Evaluate: express opinion, judge, defend/criticize | Teachers know each child and create a community of learners who support each other<br><br>Children work collaboratively<br><br>Teachers respect children's opinions and ways of thinking<br><br>Classroom environment enhances learning through thoughtful arrangement of furniture and knowledge of each child's learning style |
|---|---|---|---|---|---|---|

*(Continued)*

**TABLE 4.3** (Continued)

| Stage | Skill sets | Learning expectations | Scaffolding strategies | Access prior knowledge | Asking good/meaningful/ probing questions (Strasser & Mufson Bresson, 2017) | DAP (NAEYC, 2020) |
|---|---|---|---|---|---|---|
| | | Incorporate assistive technology as appropriate for children with special needs and/or developmental delays<br><br>Record children's stories<br><br>Explore digital storytelling<br><br>Share e-books<br><br>Use digital microscopes<br><br>Video-conferencing software<br><br>Arrange play experiences for children to construct and explore their ideas about how technology works<br><br>Provide access to photographs and experiences children may not otherwise encounter | | | Create: make, construct, design, author | Learning environment supports exploration, initiative, positive peer interaction and cognitive growth |

**TABLE 4.4** Arts Grid for technology

| Stage | Theater/drama/puppets | Music | Singing | Movement/dance | Visual arts | Creative writing | Photography/film |
|---|---|---|---|---|---|---|---|
| Toddler: 13–36 months | Simple play – games<br>Finger play<br>Puppet play<br>Poetry/poems | Simple percussion<br>Clapping<br>Patting legs or other body parts or floor<br>Themed music | Nursery rhymes<br>Songs that repeat and build<br>Dynamics of song – high/low, loud, soft, quick/slow | Simple movement actions<br>Different types of movement<br>Different dynamics<br>Fast, slow | Exploring shapes and lines<br>Exploring marks on paper<br>Exploring color<br>Exploring types of paint application – finger paints, or painting with other items | Placing marks on paper representative or symbolic for concepts, concrete ideas, or objects<br>Simple stories dictated to an adult or simple stories with symbolic marks representative of ideas or objects<br>Poetry/poems | Record either with a camera or video events, objects of meaning, or places<br>Photograph projects for sharing |
| Preschool: 3–5 years | Simple play – games<br>Finger play<br>Puppet play<br>Act out a short story<br>Poetry/poems | Simple percussion<br>Clapping<br>Patting legs or other body parts or floor<br>Themed music | Nursery rhymes<br>Songs that repeat and build<br>Dynamics of song – high/low, loud, soft, quick/slow | Simple movement actions<br>Different types of movement<br>Different dynamics<br>Fast, slow<br>Move to sound or music<br>Circle dance – follow directions | Exploring shapes and lines<br>Exploring marks on paper<br>Exploring color<br>Creating new colors | Placing marks on paper representative or symbolic for concepts, concrete ideas, or objects | Record either with a camera or video events, objects of meaning, or places<br>Photograph projects for sharing<br>Child begins to use camera and video |

(Continued)

**TABLE 4.4** (Continued)

| Stage | Theater/drama/puppets | Music | Singing | Movement/dance | Visual arts | Creative writing | Photography/film |
|---|---|---|---|---|---|---|---|
| | | | | (move in, move out, walk slowly holding hands in a circle, and so on) | Exploring types of paint application – finger paints, or painting with other items<br><br>Share art of professionals and illustrators | Simple stories dictated to an adult or simple stories with symbolic marks representative of ideas or objectsContinue to develop writing skills and story-making<br><br>Poetry/poems | |
| Kindergarten: 5–6 years | Simple play – games<br>Finger play<br>Puppet play<br>Act out a short story<br>Take a favorite story and devise a play<br>Begin to incorporate the other arts into drama | Simple percussion<br>Clapping<br>Patting legs or other body parts or floor<br>Themed music<br>Introduce instruments for playing-tambourine, sticks, drums | Nursery rhymes<br>Songs that repeat and build<br>Dynamics of song – high/low, loud, soft, quick/slow | Simple movement actions<br>Different types of movement<br>Different dynamics<br>Fast, slow<br>Move to different sounds or different types of music<br>Circle dance – follow directions | Exploring shapes and lines<br>Exploring marks on paper<br>Exploring color<br>Creating new colors<br>Exploring types of paint application – finger paints, or painting with other items | Placing marks on paper representative or symbolic for concepts, concrete ideas, or objects<br>Simple stories dictated to an adult or simple stories with symbolic marks representative of ideas or objects | Record either with a camera or video events, objects of meaning, or places<br>Photograph projects for sharing<br>Child begins to use camera and video<br>Film a play, dance, music performance, an art exhibit |

| | | | | | | |
|---|---|---|---|---|---|---|
| Act out songs<br>Songs with repetition for acting<br>Poetry/poems | Create simple clapping patterns or rhythms for children to copy and add on to<br>Find objects in the room or outside to use for percussion or rhythm | Introduce more complex songs with refrains, chorus, and different verses<br>Imitate, extend songs<br>Act out songs<br>Songs with repetition for acting | (move in, move out, walk slowly holding hands in a circle, and so on)<br>Begin to develop more complex movement actions<br>Fast, slow, high, low, twist, straight, curvy, with a partner, solo, in a group, move in, move out and so on<br>Teach folk dances or improvise a dance to a well-known and liked song | Share art of professionals<br>Art exploration with different mediums, different forms of expression, different materials, different goals | Continue to develop writing skills and story-making<br>Create stories with a beginning, middle, and end<br>Text with illustrations<br>Share writings<br>Poetry – create, share and respond to | Record either with a camera or video events, objects of meaning, or places<br>Photograph projects for sharing<br>Child begins to use camera and video<br>Film a play, dance, music performance, an art exhibit |
| **Primary Grades: 6–8 years**<br>Puppet play<br>Act out a short story<br>Take a favorite story and devise a play<br>Begin to incorporate the other arts into drama<br>Act out songs<br>Songs with repetition for acting | Simple percussion<br>Clapping<br>Patting legs or other body parts or floor<br>Themed music<br>Introduce instruments for playing – tambourine, sticks, drums | Nursery rhymes<br>Songs that repeat and build<br>Dynamics of song – high/low, loud, soft, quick/slow<br>Introduce more complex songs with refrains, chorus, and different verses | Simple movement actions<br>Different types of movement<br>Different dynamics<br>Fast, slow<br>Move to different sounds or different types of music<br>Circle dance – follow directions (move in, move out, walk slowly holding hands in a circle, and so on) | Art exploration with different mediums, different forms of expression, different materials, different goals<br>Continue to explore art from different perspectives, mediums, and themes | Create stories with a beginning, middle, and end<br>Text with illustrations<br>Share writings<br>Poetry – read, create, share<br>Stories reflect themes with complexity of action, characters, and message | |

(Continued)

**TABLE 4.4** (Continued)

| Stage | Theater/drama/puppets | Music | Singing | Movement/dance | Visual arts | Creative writing | Photography/film |
|---|---|---|---|---|---|---|---|
| | Participate in a play<br><br>Choose a theme and write a play centered around the chosen theme<br><br>Choose a theme and improvise a story | Create simple clapping patterns or rhythms for children to copy and add on to<br><br>Find objects in the room or outside to use for percussion or rhythm<br><br>Continue to develop complexity in music and use of instruments with the addition of voice and movement | Imitate, extend songs<br><br>Act out songs<br><br>Songs with repetition for acting<br><br>Continue to develop complexity in song format and style<br><br>Layer onto music and drama | Begin to develop more complex movement actions<br><br>Fast, slow, high, low, twist, straight, curvy, with a partner, solo, in a group, move in, move out, and so on<br><br>Teach folk dances or improvise a dance to a well-known and liked song<br><br>Continue to develop complexity in movement and dance<br><br>Add movement and dance to drama, music, and song | | | Continue to explore ways of using film and video |

# 5

# Young Builders Take on Engineering in Early Childhood Education

## Introduction

### Engineering
Identify a problem, design a solution, build, test, assess, re-design, build, and test.

### How Engineering Connects to Early Childhood Education
We can see from young children's play how engineering is closely integrated into early experiences and explorations. Young learners engage with materials made available in the classroom and often will find ways to create shapes, structures, and collections with the accessible items. Putting different things together in a specific or random manner teaches the child about the different qualities of the materials and how they respond to the push/pull of shape, space, and gravity. Experimenting with different designs provides hands-on constructivist learning experiences for children as they experiment with ways of putting things together.

Childen are master engineers when working with sand, mud, water, rocks, or any natural material available to them.

DOI: 10.4324/9781003395614-5

We often see our young engineers digging, constructing, organizing items for waterways, bridges, castles, houses, and canals to name a few construction projects. They have an idea (or identify a problem, e.g., this sandbox needs a canal with water), decide on the best method for achieving their idea (design a solution, e.g. use the shovel to dig the canal), dig (building on experience in the process – was the shovel method successful?), run water through the new canal (test – will the canal hold water?). This is likely followed by analysis: did it do what the engineeer wanted? (assess – the water did not run through the canal, it was soaked up by the sand), after which a child may try a different way to make the canal (re-design, e.g. will a bigger shovel work or are more diggers – classmates – needed?), and so on. Once we have named this sequence of events (engineering), we can see how busy young childen are being engineers.

We know how valuable young children's play is for learning, experimenting, and testing. Creative play for young children provides many engineering design opportunities. Most play areas in the classroom and outside are possible engineering sites. Using a sand box, or building blocks, or excavating outside in the dirt or sand, or building different configurations with available objects can all help children see when a problem arises (e.g., the structure falls down), after which they try again by creating a new design (different arrangement of objects), then see if it falls down again (test), re-assess, and re-design, continuing the process depending on the outcome of each construction effort. Outdoor spaces such as Playscapes®, or natural environments with places to dig, streams or other water sources for children to explore and experiment with supply young explorers with the means to really expand their imaginations through engineering practices.

## Engineering Design

### Defining and Delimiting an Engineering Problem

To understand a building or design problem, children ask questions to help clarify where things did not meet their expectations. When teachers ask meaningful and thoughtful questions, children are able to reflect on the situation. By asking others, children can also begin to see where their building plan did not address the problem – questions such as, *"Where did the water go in the canal?,"* or *"Why did the building fall over,?"* or an observation such as *"I can't get the ball to keep from rolling away."* Observations by the young engineers can be solicited of children regarding their building design and information is collected with the support of the teacher to help inform builders about their design strategy. What is the problem needing to be solved, and how simple or complicated is it? Teachers can help learners understand the fundamentals of a problem so a solution can be imagined. The engineering process is a way to envision how to go about organizing ideas, possible methods, materials, and solutions. This process can be very simple, or more complex, depending on your learners, the problem at hand, their prior knowledge, time, materials, and interest.

See Table 5.1 for examples of asking meaningful questions of your engineers.

See Table 5.2 for examples of engineering activities.

The following is a set of three related lesson plans for young children. The first two plans focus on introducing the concept of

**TABLE 5.1** Asking meaningful questions: engineering

| Actions | Questions |
| --- | --- |
| Remember: identify, name, repeat, recall | What is the problem you need to solve? |
| Understand: describe, discuss, explain, summarize | Can you explain what the problem is? |
| Apply: explain why, dramatize, identify with/relate to | Why is this a problem? |
| Analyze: recognize change, experiment, infer, compare, contrast | What needs to happen to solve this problem? |
| Evaluate: express opinion, judge, defend/criticize | Did it work, was the problem solved? |
| Create: make, construct, design, author | Can you create another design to solve a different problem? |

**TABLE 5.2** Engineering activities

| Engineering tasks | Activities and creative arts |
|---|---|
| Identify a problem | Blocks: Free exploration with blocks. Identify a problem: use only the rectangular blocks to build a tower to a certain height |
| Design a solution | Rectangular blocks used one way are not enough. Rectangular block used end to end (long way) meet the requirements |
| Build | |
| Test | Build, test, assess, re-design if necessary |
| Assess | Provide a select number, shape or size of block. |
| Re-design | Free exploration: see what happens with the select type of blocks. |
| Test again | |

Identify a problem: using all the blocks available, create a structure meeting certain specifications appropriate to the circumstances, child, and skill set of the child.

Design a solution, build, test, assess, re-design if necessary

Ask meaningful questions: observe children using blocks. Ask probing questions about their activities, *"What can you tell me about what you are working on?"*

Let the builders identify problems they might be having and then ask questions to lead them into reflecting on their process, *"What happens if ...?," "Do you think ...?"*

Sand/water table:

Provide a variety of objects for children to use with the sand or water to construct, arrange, build, or design

Ask meaningful questions: observe children at the sand/water table. Ask probing questions about their activities, *"What can you tell me about what you are working on?"*

Let the designers identify problems they might be having and then ask questions to lead them into reflecting on their process, *"What happens if ...?," "Do you think ...?"*

Outdoor play space (e.g., Playscapes®):

This is a rich environment for engineering exploration and experimentation. Make sure there are many objects provided for moving, rearranging, and building. Children will identify problems such as an area needing seats for play, a hole for water or sand, a lookout for a specific type of dramatic play. In outside settings with lots of options such as are available in playscapes, children will naturally engage in engineering practices.

**TABLE 5.2** (*Continued*)

| Engineering tasks | Activities and creative arts |
| --- | --- |
| | Construction project: |
| | This activity can be done with any curriculum area or topic of investigation. We will focus on the use of recycled items with a specific goal or problem to solve. |
| | Provide specific recycled items for use |
| | With the specific objects in mind, pose a building/creating challenge |
| | Recycled items: |
| | *Use your objects to construct …* |
| | *All the items must be used in your project.* |
| | See what happens |
| | Music: Fun and creative activity – build an instrument which makes or does something specified. It needs to be achievable by the children with materials provided. |
| | Something you can beat on like a drum |
| | Something to strum like a guitar or violin |
| | Something which will make a sound when you blow on it or through a small air tunnel like a flute or recorder |
| | Dance: Use bodies to create a designated shape or form |
| | Theater: Using a story or poem with an engineering focus, create a simple dramatic presentation |
| | *Imagine a Day; Imagine a Night; Imagine a World* by Sarah L. Thompson. These are wonderful fantasy books where the world becomes topsy-turvy through children's imaginations as they imagine different ways to live, see, experience, and be. Makes for fun dramatic representations. |

engineering. The second lesson plan develops the engineering process. The concluding lesson revisits the explorations in engineering and provides opportunity for the children to explore the engineering process.

# Engineering Design: Lesson Plan Model – Introduction

- ◆ *Age range*: 4–6 years old: preschool/kindergarten.
- ◆ *Instructional objective*: Introduce the children to the idea of engineering.

◆ *Learning target*: Through whole-class discussion access their prior knowledge regarding what they might know about engineering. Introduce the process and write the words up where the children are able to see them.

◆ *Open-ended question*: Introduce the word "Engineering." *"What is engineering? What do you know about engineering?"* Follow-up response – *"Tell me more about it."*

◆ Record their ideas on chart paper or use a whiteboard.

◆ Read an engineering story: here are some possibilities:
   ◆ *The Most Magnificent Thing* by Ashley Spires
   ◆ *When I Build with Blocks* by Niki Alling
   ◆ *Be a Maker* by Katey Howes
   ◆ *Imagine a Day* by Sarah L. Thompson
   ◆ *Imagine a Night* by Sarah L. Thompson
   ◆ *Brick by Brick* by Heidi Woodward Sheffield
   ◆ *If I Build A House* by Chris Van Dusen

◆ Open-ended questions about the story which was read to the class.
   ◆ *What did you notice about the story?*
   ◆ *Tell me more …*
   ◆ *What were the characters' ideas about building and engineering?*
   ◆ *What engineering activities happened in the story?*
   ◆ *What do you think about the way the story ended?*
   ◆ *Tell me more …*

◆ Record children's ideas and responses on chart paper or a whiteboard.

◆ Review them before ending this introduction lesson on engineering design.

◆ Assessment:
   ◆ Were all the children engaged?
   ◆ Were all the children able to participate?

◆ Modifications: ensure all children are able to participate as is appropriate for each child.
   ◆ Knowledge of each child
   ◆ Teacher support with physical components of project
   ◆ One-on-one with child.

◆ Developmentally Appropriate Practice:
  ◆ *Families*: Reach out to families prior to the lessons to see if there are any experts or resources. Also let the families know what their child will be doing in class for a few days.
  ◆ *Intentional teaching*: Ask thoughtful, child-centric, open-ended questions, support all learners where they are developmentally

## Engineering Design: Lesson Plan – Development

◆ *Age range*: 4–6 years old: preschool/kindergarten.
◆ *Learning target*: Develop engineering ideas from the first lesson through hands-on, open-ended exploration using specific items provided by the teacher along with teacher support and scaffolding when appropriate.
  ◆ Review the first lesson's chart list from the introductory discussion on engineering along with the ideas generated by the children from the story they read.
◆ *Directions*: the children will explore designing and building using a variety of materials provided for this activity.
  ◆ Materials for exploration, experimentation, and building.
  ◆ Recycled items such as: plastic containers, cardboard, cardboard tubes, plastic trays, take-out containers, cups, large and small cylindrical containers (oatmeal containers), different types of scrap paper, toothpicks, small plastic items.
  ◆ Large items which are recycled such as tubs, buckets, large boxes.
  ◆ String, ribbon, yarn, material.
◆ Allow the children to explore the different materials.
◆ Provide each child with a large piece of cardboard on which they can build their creation.
◆ Use open-ended questions to help the children reflect, process, and explain their ideas.

- ◆ Allow ample time for children to explore, experiment, test, assess, and try again.
- ◆ Bring the class together after a designated period of time to share their process and outcomes.
- ◆ Asking probing and thoughtful questions:
  - ◆ *Tell me about your design.*
  - ◆ *How did you decide what to use?*
  - ◆ *Tell me more …*
  - ◆ *How well did your building or creation stay up? Was there any rebuilding you needed to do? Tell me more …*
- ◆ As time allows, let each child share and explain about their project.
- ◆ Assessment:
  - ◆ Were all the children engaged?
  - ◆ Were the math principles of engineering applied?
  - ◆ Were all the children able to participate?
- ◆ Modifications: ensure all children are able to participate as is appropriate for each child:
  - ◆ Knowledge of each child
  - ◆ Teacher support with physical components of project
  - ◆ One-on-one with child.
- ◆ Developmentally appropriate practice:
  - ◆ *Families*: Share with families the activities of the day.
  - ◆ *Intentional teaching*: Ask thoughtful, child-centric, open-ended questions, support all learners where they are developmentally.

## Engineering Design: Lesson Plan Model – Conclusion

- ◆ *Age range*: 4–6 years old: preschool/kindergarten.
- ◆ *Learning target*: Introduce the engineering process using their building experience from the previous lesson along with ideas from an engineering book of choice.
- ◆ Read another engineering/building story.
- ◆ Use open-ended and probing questions to discover the engineering process used in the story:
  - ◆ *How did the main character go about deciding what to build?*

- ◆ *Tell me what you noticed when the main character decided to build a house for her dog (or whatever else the main character built). What were the steps she went through as she decided how to build her dog a house?*
  - ◆ *What else did you notice?*
- ◆ Help the children identify the engineering process in the story. Did any of them experience some or all of that process while building during the previous lesson? Ask them to explain.
- ◆ Finish sharing projects from the previous lesson if need be.
- ◆ Review the process once more with the class.
- ◆ Take photos of the projects for display and sharing with families.
- ◆ Assessment:
  - ◆ Were all the children engaged?
  - ◆ Were the children able to discuss the process they went through to build their structure or creation?
  - ◆ Were all the children able to participate?
- ◆ Modifications: ensure all children are able to participate as is appropriate for each child.
  - ◆ Knowledge of each child
  - ◆ Teacher support with physical components of project
  - ◆ One-on-one with child.
- ◆ Developmentally Appropriate Practice:
  - ◆ *Families*: Share with families the activities of the day.
  - ◆ *Intentional teaching*: Ask thoughtful, child-centric, open-ended questions, support all learners where they are developmentally.

Table 5.3 shows an engineering grid of skill sets and DAP, and Table 5.4 shows suggested themes/topics for arts and engineering. It presents the materials available for exploration and construction, the space for engineering activities, the literature featuring the engineering process (i.e., identify a problem, design a solution, build, test assess, redesign, etc.) (see *Imagine a Day* by Sarah Thomson), and offers an opportunity to implement the engineering process.

**TABLE 5.3** Engineering Grid of skill sets and DAP

| Stage | Skill sets | Learning expectations | Scaffolding strategies | Access prior knowledge | Asking good/meaningful/ probing questions | DAP (NAEYC, 2020) |
|---|---|---|---|---|---|---|
| Toddler: 13–36 months | Dependence on adults<br>Learning to speak<br>Coordinate sensations and physical activities<br>Think with symbols<br>Imitate and learn from others (Santrock, 2019) | Engagement<br>Interest<br>Exploration<br>Asking questions<br>Free exploration of materials | Verbal encouragement<br>Demonstration<br>Physical support<br>Patience | Observation<br>Asking probing questions<br>Being an attentive listener | *Levels of questioning and expected response or behavior from the child*<br>Remember: identify, name, count, repeat, recall<br>Understand: describe, discuss, explain, summarize<br>Apply: Explain why, dramatize, identify with/relate to<br>Analyze: recognize change, experiment, infer, compare, contrast<br>Evaluate: express opinion, judge, defend/criticize<br>Create: make, construct, design, author | Relationship with primary caregiver established as warm and welcoming<br>Learn toddler's ways and habits from observation and interactions<br>Acceptance and adjust to toddler's ways and preferences<br>Responsive to toddler's needs<br>Environment appropriate for the toddler with different spaces (quiet, play, small group, individual), with toys to manipulate and explore<br>Indoor and outdoor spaces |

| Preschool: 3–5 years | | | *Levels of questioning and expected response or behavior from the child* | |
|---|---|---|---|---|
| Curriculum and activities enhances development – physical (small and gross motor), social and emotional, and cognitive (language: listening, speaking, and understanding) | Asking questions | Observation | Remember: identify, name, count, repeat, recall | Foster positive relationships |
| Reading and writing (attendant skills | Observation | Asking probing questions | Understand: describe, discuss, explain, summarize | Build classroom community |
| Curiosity about the world around them | Verbal encouragement | Being an attentive listener | Apply: Explain why, dramatize, identify with/relate to | Safe, healthy environment promotes independence and exploration w/clear boundaries |
| Engagement, exploration, experimentation, and observation | Demonstration | Use of a KWL chart or something similar | Analyze: recognize change, experiment, infer, compare, contrast | Spaces promote variety of learning opportunities: small group, large group, individual |
| Engagement with building materials and activities | Physical support | | Evaluate: express opinion, judge, defend / criticize | Different areas arranged to promote different learning styles |
| Introduction to engineering process and language: identify a problem, design a solution, build, test, assess, redesign | Patience | | Create: make, construct, design, author | |
| | Adult or peer demonstrates skill set | | | |

*(Continued)*

**TABLE 5.3** (Continued)

| Stage | Skill sets | Learning expectations | Scaffolding strategies | Access prior knowledge | Asking good/meaningful/ probing questions | DAP (NAEYC, 2020) |
|---|---|---|---|---|---|---|
| Kindergarten: 5–6 years | Curriculum and activities enhances development – physical (small and gross motor), social and emotional, and cognitive (language: listening, speaking, and understanding)<br><br>Reading and writing (attendant skills)<br><br>Develop vocabulary– language of engineering | Curiosity about the world around them<br><br>Engagement with exploration, experimentation, and observation<br><br>Provide materials for exploration, manipulation, and experimentation<br><br>Explore engineering process and language: identify a problem, design a solution, build, test, assess, redesign<br><br>Use drawings and models to demonstrate problem and solution | Asking questions<br><br>Observation<br><br>Verbal encouragement<br><br>Demonstration<br><br>Physical support<br><br>Patience<br><br>Adult or peer demonstrates skill set<br><br>Model process: Identify a problem, design a solution collaboratively | Observation<br><br>Asking probing questions<br><br>Being an attentive listener<br><br>Use of a KWL chart or something similar | *Levels of questioning and expected response or behavior from the child*<br><br>Remember: identify, name, count, repeat, recall<br><br>Understand: describe, discuss, explain, summarize<br><br>Apply: Explain why, dramatize, identify with/relate to<br><br>Analyze: recognize change, experiment, infer, compare, contrast<br><br>Evaluate: express opinion, judge, defend/criticize<br><br>Create: make, construct, design, author | Foster positive relationships<br><br>Build classroom community<br><br>Learning environment promotes exploration, initiative, positive peer interaction, and cognitive growth<br><br>Spaces promote variety of learning opportunities: small group, large group, individual<br><br>Different areas arranged to promote different learning styles |

| | | | Asking questions | Observation | *Levels of questioning and expected response or behavior from the child* | |
|---|---|---|---|---|---|---|
| Primary Grades: 6–8 years | Curriculum and activities enhances development – physical (small and gross motor), social and emotional, and cognitive (language: listening, speaking, and understanding, word and print knowledge, phonemic awareness) Reading and writing (attendant skills) Develop vocabulary – language of engineering | Engagement with exploration, experimentation, and observation Provide materials for exploration, manipulation, and experimentation Investigate through hands-on the engineering process: identify a problem, design a solution, build, test, assess, redesign Use drawings and models to demonstrate problem and solution | Asking questions Observation Verbal encouragement Demonstration Physical support Patience Adult or peer demonstrates skill set Model process: Identify a problem, design a solution collaboratively | Observation Asking probing questions Being an attentive listener Use of a KWL chart or something similar | Remember: identify, name, count, repeat, recall Understand: describe, discuss, explain, summarize Apply: Explain why, dramatize, identify with/relate to Analyze: recognize change, experiment, infer, compare, contrast Evaluate: express opinion, judge, defend/criticize Create: make, construct, design, author | Teachers know each child and create a community of learners who support each other Children work collaboratively Teachers respect children's opinions and ways of thinking Classroom environment enhances learning through thoughtful arrangement of furniture and knowledge of each child's learning style Learning environment supports exploration, initiative, positive peer interaction and cognitive growth |

**TABLE 5.4** Art Grid and engineering

| Stage | Theater/drama | Music | Singing | Movement/dance | Visual arts | Creative writing | Photography/film |
|---|---|---|---|---|---|---|---|
| Toddler: 13–36 months | Simple play – games<br>Finger play<br>Puppet play<br>Poetry / poems | Simple percussion<br>Clapping<br>Patting legs or other body parts or floor<br>Themed music | Nursery rhymes<br>Songs that repeat and build<br>Dynamics of song – high / low, loud, soft, quick / slow | Simple movement actions<br>Different types of movement<br>Different dynamics<br>Fast, slow | Exploring shapes and lines<br>Exploring marks on paper<br>Exploring color<br>Exploring types of paint application – finger paints, or painting with other items | Placing marks on paper representative or symbolic for concepts, concrete ideas, or objects<br>Simple stories dictated to an adult or simple stories with symbolic marks representative of ideas or objects<br>Poetry / poems | Record either with a camera or video events, objects of meaning, or places<br>Photograph projects for sharing |
| Preschool: 3–5 years | Simple play – games<br>Finger play<br>Puppet play<br>Act out a short story<br>Poetry / poems | Simple percussion<br>Clapping<br>Patting legs or other body parts or floor<br>Themed music | Nursery rhymes<br>Songs that repeat and build<br>Dynamics of song – high / low, loud, soft, quick / slow | Simple movement actions<br>Different types of movement<br>Different dynamics<br>Fast, slow<br>Move to sound or music<br>Circle dance – follow directions (move in, move out, walk slowly holding hands in a circle, and so on) | Exploring shapes and lines<br>Exploring marks on paper<br>Exploring color<br>Creating new colors<br>Exploring types of paint application – finger paints, or painting with other items<br>Share art of professionals and illustrators | Placing marks on paper representative or symbolic for concepts, concrete ideas, or objects<br>Simple stories dictated to an adult or simple stories with symbolic marks representative of ideas or objects<br>Continue to develop writing skills and story-making<br>Poetry / poems | Record either with a camera or video events, objects of meaning, or places<br>Photograph projects for sharing<br>Child begins to use camera and video |

(Continued)

| Kindergarten: 5–6 years | | | | | | | |
|---|---|---|---|---|---|---|---|
| Simple play – games | Simple percussion | Nursery rhymes | Simple movement actions | Exploring shapes and lines | Placing marks on paper representative or symbolic for concepts, concrete ideas, or objects | Record either with a camera or video events, objects of meaning, or places | |
| Finger play | Clapping | Songs that repeat and build | Different types of movement | Exploring marks on paper | | Photograph projects for sharing | |
| Puppet play | Patting legs or other body parts or floor | Dynamics of song – high/low, loud, soft, quick/slow | Different dynamics | Exploring color | Simple stories dictated to an adult or simple stories with symbolic marks representative of ideas or objects | Child begins to use camera and video | |
| Act out a short story | Themed music | Introduce more complex songs with refrains, chorus, and different verses | Fast, slow | Creating new colors | | Film a play, dance, music performance, an art exhibit | |
| Take a favorite story and devise a play | Introduce instruments for playing – tambourine, sticks, drums | •Imitate, extend songs | Move to different sounds or different types of music | Exploring types of paint application – finger paints, or painting with other items | Continue to develop writing skills and story-making | | |
| Begin to incorporate the other arts into drama | Create simple clapping patterns or rhythms for children to copy and add on to | Act out songs | Circle dance – follow directions | | Create stories with a beginning, middle, and end | | |
| Act out songs | Find objects in the room or outside to use for percussion or rhythm | Songs with repetition for acting | (move in, move out, walk slowly holding hands in a circle, and so on) | Share art of professionals | Text with illustrations | | |
| Songs with repetition for acting | | | Begin to develop more complex movement actions | Art exploration with different mediums, different forms of expression, different materials, different goals | Share writings | | |
| Poetry/poems | | | Fast, slow, high, low, twist, straight, curvy, with a partner, solo, in a group, move in, move out and so on | | Poetry – create, share and respond to | | |
| | | | Teach folk dances or improvise a dance to a well-known and liked song | | | | |

**TABLE 5.4** (Continued)

| Stage | Theater/drama | Music | Singing | Movement/dance | Visual arts | Creative writing | Photography/film |
|---|---|---|---|---|---|---|---|
| Primary Grades: 6–8 years | Puppet play<br><br>Act out a short story<br><br>Take a favorite story and devise a play<br><br>Begin to incorporate the other arts into drama<br><br>Act out songs<br><br>Songs with repetition for acting<br><br>Participate in a play<br><br>Choose a theme and write a play centered around the chosen theme | Simple percussion<br><br>Clapping<br><br>Patting legs or other body parts or floor<br><br>Themed music<br><br>Introduce instruments for playing – tambourine, sticks, drums<br><br>Create simple clapping patterns or rhythms for children to copy and add on to<br><br>Find objects in the room or outside to use for percussion or rhythm | Nursery rhymes<br><br>Songs that repeat and build<br><br>Dynamics of song – high/low, loud, soft, quick/slow<br><br>Introduce more complex songs with refrains, chorus, and different verses<br><br>Imitate, extend songs<br><br>Act out songs<br><br>Songs with repetition for acting | Simple movement actions<br><br>Different types of movement<br><br>Different dynamics<br><br>Fast, slow<br><br>Move to different sounds or different types of music<br><br>Circle dance – follow directions<br><br>(move in, move out, walk slowly holding hands in a circle, and so on)<br><br>Begin to develop more complex movement actions<br><br>Fast, slow, high, low, twist, straight, curvy, with a partner, solo, in a group, move in, move out and so on | Art exploration with different mediums, different forms of expression, different materials, different goals<br><br>Continue to explore art from different perspectives, mediums, and themes | Create stories with a beginning, middle, and end<br><br>Text with illustrations<br><br>Share writings<br><br>Poetry – read, create, share<br><br>Stories reflect themes with complexity of action, characters, and message | Record either with a camera or video events, objects of meaning, or places<br><br>Photograph projects for sharing<br><br>Child begins to use camera and video<br><br>Film a play, dance, music performance, an art exhibit<br><br>•Continue to explore ways of using film and video |

| | | | |
|---|---|---|---|
| Choose a theme and improvise a story | Continue to develop complexity in music and use of instruments with the addition of voice and movement | Continue to develop complexity in song format and style<br>Layer onto and dram | Teach folk dances or improvise a dance to a well-known and liked song<br>Continue to develop complexity in movement and dance<br>Add movement and dance to drama, music, and song |

# 6

# A Child's World View Through Mathematics

## Introduction

### Teaching Math in Early Childhood

Young children, toddlers, and infants are immersed in experiences with numbers, size, and other mathematic concepts that define their world every day. The interest and ability to learn math on a somewhat more formal basis are present in children's lives from the youngest age on. They experience a sense of magnitude, they compare and contrast, they count, they evaluate observable data, they sort, organize, group, and classify. Math is integral to helping young children see, interact with, and make sense of their world. Children are adept at evaluating size and amount – *that cookie is smaller than mine*, or *there are more grapes on that plate than mine*. Or simply "I want more!" Studies of young children's math experiences and later skill acquisitions have demonstrated a connection between early math experiences and later success in both mathematics and reading (Clements & Sarama, 2014), so we know that mathematics is integral to much more than just comparing and counting.

This chapter covers math skills supported by research and practices of a variety of national math organizations. Much of the

DOI: 10.4324/9781003395614-6

research referenced is from the work of Douglas H. Clemens and Julie Sarama, who have extensively studied young children's mathematical understandings while using an approach they call "learning trajectories," discussed later in this chapter. The Erikson Institute Early Math Collaborative is another primary source of math practices you will find cited throughout this chapter. Also referenced is the *Childhood Encyclopedia of Child Development* www.child-encyclopedia.com/. Finally, the work of the National Council of Teachers of Mathematics (NCTM) is highlighted. There is a lot to cover in this chapter, so let's begin.

## Standards

State departments of education will have math standards usually based on national standards. The NCTM Principles for School Mathematics standards are a good example and are summarized here:

◆ *Equity*: Excellence in mathematics education requires equally high expectations and strong support for all students.
◆ *Curriculum*: A curriculum is more than a collection of activities; it must be coherent, focused on important mathematics, and well-articulated across the grades.
◆ *Teaching*: Effective mathematics teaching requires understanding of what students know and need to learn and then challenging and supporting them to learn it well.
◆ *Learning*: Students must learn mathematics with understanding, actively building new knowledge from experience and prior knowledge (learning to think mathematically)
◆ *Assessment*: Assessment should support the learning of important mathematics and furnish useful information to both teachers and students.
◆ *Technology*: Technology is essential to teaching and learning mathematics; it influences the mathematics that is taught and enhancers students' learning.

Enhance children's natural interest in mathematics while building on their prior knowledge – their experiences, and what they believe they know. As you develop curriculum, be guided by your knowledge of young children's cognitive, linguistic, physical, and social and emotional development.

As you plan your math curriculum, focus on a range of skills, content, and goals for your young learners. Be guided by what your children know, their developmental stage, standards, and practices described in this chapter. Use curriculum and teaching practices that strengthen children's problem-solving and reasoning processes as well as representing, communicating, and connecting mathematical ideas. Asking meaningful, open-ended questions fosters reflection, inquiry skills, and scaffolds children's learning. Listening carefully to your students' responses and observing their actions informs you as the teacher about their problem-solving and reasoning process. A number of central mathematical ideas are a focal part of this chapter. Activities and teaching methods that strengthen children's problem-solving and reasoning processes are further central to a curriculum which also allows children to work on ways that math ideas can be represented, communicated, and connected. A constructivist learning environment that includes a scaffolding approach to young children's experiences allows your future mathematicians to grow and thrive.

Math is a natural part of what all children do throughout their day. It then makes sense to integrate mathematics with other activities and other activities with mathematics. We don't always build adequate time into the scholastic day for children to play, explore, test, and manipulate. For children to engage fully in play, ample time is needed. This time allotment will provide the context in which they explore and manipulate mathematical ideas with teacher support. Actively introduce mathematical concepts, methods, and language through a range of appropriate experiences and teaching strategies. Support children's learning by thoughtfully and continually assessing all children's mathematical knowledge and strategies through careful observation and thoughtful questioning.

Key points for educators of young children to know and understand when working with students are characteristics which are germane to the age of the student and how best to promote meaningful learning and development. Each child is unique in their development; teachers should strive to ensure that the experience of learning is able to meet each child's needs. Know your student's home and community, their social and cultural experience. The child's family is your best resource for each young learner.

## Developmentally Appropriate Practice (DAP) and Math in Early Childhood

We know the value of early literacy for young children. There is much evidence supporting the importance of reading to young children, of being around books, and having language (written and spoken) as an integral part of a child's life. Like the teaching of early literacy, mathematics education in the early childhood years is key to increasing all children's school readiness and to closing the achievement gap. Within the mathematics arena, preschoolers' knowledge of numbers and their sequence, for example, strongly predicts not only math learning but also literacy skills. Yet mathematics typically gets little attention before kindergarten. One reason is that early childhood teachers themselves often lack the confidence and know-how to substantially and effectively increase their attention to mathematics in the curriculum.

Mathematics and literacy concepts and skills and, indeed, robust content across the curriculum, can be taught to young children in ways that are appealing and developmentally appropriate. The NAEYC guidelines for this approach are summarized here (NAEYC, 2020):

- ◆ Creating a caring, equitable community of learners.
- ◆ Engaging in reciprocal partnerships with families and fostering community connections.
- ◆ Observing, documenting, and assessing children's development and learning.
- ◆ Teaching to enhance each child's development and learning.
- ◆ Planning and implementing an engaging curriculum to achieve meaningful goals.
- ◆ Demonstrating professionalism as an Early Childhood Educator.

The following sections of this chapter go into the different areas of a comprehensive and thoughtful math program for young children. This information is organized in a skill-based hierarchical configuration so that the early topics are key to laying a strong and secure foundation for later math investigations and skill sets. This process starts with numeracy and the amazing abilities of very young children, even babies in fact, to discern differences in quantities.

## Numeracy and Counting

### The Transition from Infancy to Early Childhood and Numerical Knowledge in Early Childhood

The effective inclusion of numeracy in early childhood education can help to develop children's sense of number, strategies to solve number problems, and an awareness of how numbers can help to make sense of their world.

Number concepts have been shown to emerge in the very early stages of life. Infants have demonstrated a sensitivity to nonverbal numeracy. An example of this is demonstrated in a study by Clements and Sarama (2014): "three pictures hang in front of a six-month-old child. The first shows two dots, the others one dot and three dots. The infant hears three drumbeats. Her eyes move to the picture with three dots." This is an example of an "approximate number system" (ANS) where the individual is able to detect the magnitude of a group without the use of language or symbols. This cognitive ability is present in early infancy.

Another mathematical skill important to the development of later mathematical abilities is subitizing, which is the ability to recognize the exact number of a group quickly. According to Clements and Sarama (2014), *conceptual subitizing helps children develop abstract number and arithmetic strategies.* Verbal Number Recognition (VNR) is another way to describe a child's ability to recognize and verbalize a quantity. Scaffold children's experiences with VNR by helping them to use and think of a specific quantity in a variety of different ways, e.g., reinforcing the number three by using three apples, three claps, three dots, three toys, and so on. This can also be extended by the use of thoughtful questioning into fact fluency, for instance, leveraging the notion of three of something through the addition of another of those things to the group. "You picked three apples, do you want to pick one more apple? Now how many apples do you have?"

Providing opportunities for young children to express numeracy concepts verbally is another building block in the growth and acquisition of mathematical concepts supporting the ability to understand more complex math competency in later childhood. Children are able to count in sequence before the age of 3. Counting to the number 10 can be memorized before the age of 6. Also within this 3–6 age bracket, children begin to master counting using the decade structures (e.g., counting by tens).

Provide children aged 3–3½ years with ample opportunities to experience the *one-to-one principle,* i.e., one object-one count. Between the ages of 3 and 5, children begin to recognize that the number of the last object counted in a group is the overall number of objects in that group. This is another conceptual stepping-stone to math abilities as children grow in experience and knowledge. This skill is known as the cardinality principle: if you count one, two, three apples in this set, then the total number of apples in this set is three.

## Principles of How to Count

Gelman and Gallistel (1986) present the principles of how to count.

### *One-to-One Principle*

When counting, the child is able to distinguish objects counted in a set from those not yet counted. A one-to-one correspondence is used as the child names each object counted. The child is able to touch one object in a set, say "one," touch a second object in the set, say "two," and so on until all items in the set have been counted.

### Stable Order Principle

The child when counting is able to say the same number word in the same order each time they count items in a set. *"This is one, then two, next comes three"* as they touch the item in a set and speak the number word.

### Cardinality Principle

The ability of the child to recognize that a set or group of objects can be represented by a number and that number will always be the last number spoken when counting the objects in a set or group. Four bananas counted is the number of bananas in the set.

## "What to Count" Principles

### Abstraction Principle

- ◆ Any group of objects is able to be counted.
- ◆ Objects in a group which are the same, as well as objects in that group which are different, can be counted.
  - ◆ A set of blocks which are all the same shape can be counted. A collection of blocks of all different shapes can also be counted.
  - ◆ Nontangible things can also be counted such as sounds, claps, steps, or words. Children arrive at this realization as they experience counting in different ways and counting different things.

### Order-Irrelevance Principle

Children come to understand that sets of objects can be counted in any order as long as each item in the set is included in the count.

## Early Predictors of Mathematics Achievement and Mathematics Learning Difficulties

The importance of early exposure and experience with numeracy, number sense, and number recognition has been stressed so far in this chapter. Not only is early experience with numeracy critical to children's mathematical competencies, but it can also identify children who struggle with numeracy sensitivity and awareness (Jordan, 2010). Developmental dyscalculia is a mathematics disability where the individual's ability to recognize, compute, and count numbers is compromised. The principles of how and what to count are also challenging. Pattern recognition is hard for children with dyscalculia.

Young children should be screened for math difficulties early so an intervention program can be put in place. Difficulties with mathematics at an early age can have long-term consequences for more complex mathematics later in the child's school life if left unaddressed.

## Learning Trajectories

This section describes a way to envision and plan math instruction and activities for early childhood. It is an approach developed by Clements and Sarama (2014) through their work with young children.

A learning trajectory has three components to it. The first component is identifying a mathematical goal. Goals are the "Big Ideas" of mathematics. These ideas are groups of mathcentric concepts and skills that follow children's cognitive development while supporting future learning. Big Ideas are reflected in the result of several projects carried out by National Council of Teachers of Mathematics and the Mathematics Advisory Panel among others. For example, a Big Idea is the type of counting which identifies how many in a set.

Developmental progression: the paths of learning leading to the identified goal is the second part of the learning trajectory. Knowledge of how children learn, their developmental pathways, and understanding of the mathematical skills young children are capable of acquiring guide teachers in building series of experiences and activities enhancing and supporting acquisition of the identified goal. As noted in the beginning of this chapter, counting is an essential part of acquiring numeracy skills. After identifying the mathematical goal of counting the number of items in a set, then teachers can determine the path of learning (developmental progression), which depends on each child's own learning trajectory and developmental stage with numeracy concepts.

The final part of the learning trajectory is represented in the instructional activities which provide important learning pathways. The tasks are designed to promote children's growth from one level of understanding and skill acquisition to the next level. These are different activities focusing on counting up to three or any designated number in a set. Providing different opportunities to count items focusing on the principles of how to count will be the path of learning for your young learners.

A short summary of learning trajectories includes the following:

1. Identify a goal: for example, counting which identifies how many objects in a set.
2. Establish developmental progression: How will the child achieve the goal based on his/her developmental stage and pathway?
3. Provide paths of learning through instructional activities: Identify activities, materials, and methodology of support (access prior knowledge and scaffold child as needed), and interaction with the child.

## Mathematics Is All Around Us

### Shepherd's Night Count
*Jane Yolen*

One ewe,
One ram,
Two sheep,
One flock,
Four gates,
One lock,
Five folds,
One light,
Good dog,
Good night.

"Shepherd's Night Count" by Jane Yolen is about numbers of sheep and other objects found on a sheep farm. The sheep are counted as well as the gates in the fields, the pens or folds the sheep stay in, and the light the shepherd carries to put the sheep to bed in their folds. This poem has many possibilities for creative integration into the arts in addition to its being a fun poem to read and imagine while introducing some possibly new and interesting vocabulary. Math is all around us, as this poem demonstrates.

To optimize children experiencing and exploring math concepts within their daily lives, we must cultivate a way of thinking and seeing which frames our environment in mathematical terms. Thinking mathematically informs our way of understanding the world around us in mathematical terms and concepts. The use of "manipulatives" has become a common element of many or most math curricula developed for young children. Knowing that mathematics is much, much more than manipulatives broadens our scope of awareness and guides us as teachers in our interactions with young children.

Language development also supports young children's ability to abstract ways of thinking about the world. Using language to create context around math concepts, such as comparisons, attributes, quality, quantity, sets, order, size, placement, value, and so on helps young children build knowledge of their world and mathematics' place in it.

## Math Is Everywhere

As mentioned earlier, each day of most children's lives is infused with math experiences and opportunities. Weave multi-experiential opportunities into each day capitalizing on each child's interests, skills, and developmental abilities. Children gravitate to areas in the classroom which hold attractions for them, such as the sensory tables, or block area, or the dramatic play space, or the arts area. Using the language of math such as: comparisons, attributes, quality, quantity, sets, order, size, placement, or value, teachers can engage learners in conversation with questions focused on a math concept or skill. *"How much space do you need to build your barn?," "Did you use more materials in this design than the first design?," "How many beads do you need to make a bracelet which is long enough for your wrist?,"* and so on.

## Scaffolding Children's Learning

Apply a *constructivist* approach (building on existing knowledge to learn new information) to your teaching; this approach lends itself naturally to scaffolding practices. Observing children at play or during investigative activities, you will be able to determine appropriate entry points for scaffolding your young learner to the next skill level. Scaffolding supports children who are ready to move beyond where they currently are developmentally. Scaffolding through adult or peer support moves a child beyond the boundary between one skill set and the next one. Scaffolding can include questions asked to prompt the child to reflect, a process which provides a helping hand encouraging the learner to take those next tentative steps.

Some important topics areas in the teaching of math to young children include the following (see Erikson Institute, 2014); these are developed in more detail in the following sections of the chapter.

The Erikson Institute's Topic Areas of Early Mathematics include counting which bring the topics to nine. We introduced counting earlier in this chapter so it has not been included here, making the number of topics covered here eight (Erikson Institute, 2014):

1. Sets
2. Number Sense
3. Number Operations
4. Pattern
5. Measurement
6. Data Analysis
7. Spatial Relationships
8. Shape

# Sets

The Erikson Institute defines a set as "any collection that is grouped together in some meaningful way" (Erikson Institute, 2014). A collection can be grouped by attributes of choice such as size, color, shape, or theme. Collections can share one attribute or more, depending on the focus of the activity. Further exploration with sets can delve into comparing sets, how are they the same or different? Similarities are generally easier to identify than differences, so finding shared attributes is a good place to start.

These topics are hierarchically organized based on experience and the child's understanding of sets and the relationships between them. What is developmentally appropriate for each child will inform your teaching and interactions. Ask open-ended questions about the set. Listen carefully to observations made by each child as they explore and experiment. Keep the number of variables simple to begin, such as color or category. Create opportunities for different sets to be compared and ordered in various ways, guiding the learner in different ways to see and order the objects. Focus comparisons on quantity, such as *"Do these two sets have the same or equal number of objects, or more than, or less than?"* with follow-up questions, for example, *"How do you know?"*. Ask authentic questions that are open-ended.

Activities, such as sorting and matching objects, provide children with the opportunity to begin discerning sameness and differences, based on attributes identified by the child or adult. In matching tasks, the children find the items which are the same in all ways or in ways predetermined by the teacher or child. One activity is called "Find My Match" (the child looks to find an item matching one already chosen, e.g., a green circle) focuses on the item as a whole, in this case green circles (this object has two attributes: color and shape). The child is asked to find all the green circles in the box or room, or whatever is appropriate. Sorting using a game called "What's My Rule?" can also be encouraged using specific rules which can be simple or more complex, such as all objects in the set are blue, regardless of size or shape. A more challenging activity for this game is to have all the objects in the set have a shared use, like crayons and magic markers. The greater the number of specific rules or attributes, the more challenging the task or game becomes. One attribute for a set might be shape or color. Two attributes can be color and shape or size and color. Making comparisons between objects helps children build observational skill sets –noticing similarities and differences. As in all we do in the classroom, making learning experiences meaningful creates connections for children while building understanding.

## Number Sense

Numbers help define our experiences and perceptions about our world. Create a math curriculum which provides young learners with ways in which to encounter numbers and the many ways they are used to understand and define sets. The Erikson Institute (2014) identifies three Big Ideas to inform and focus your numeracy program: (1) numbers are used in a range of ways; (2) quantity is a feature of a set of objects; and (3) the quantity of a small collection can be perceived without counting.

When planning and creating a mathematics curriculum to best meet each child's needs in an early childhood setting, the math content for meaningful learning should be central to all the activities. Awareness of how math activities are perceived and understood by your learners is important to their success with the math curriculum. The math experiences of young children should serve as a springboard for future learning. The development of number sense in young children provides a building block for more complex math, such as "fact fluency." Fact fluency is helping children identify patterns and predictability among specific groups of numbers, also known as fact families. Developing an informal number sense prior to first grade builds a foundation for formal "fact fluency" in later grades, such as $2 + 1 = 3$; $1 + 2 = 3$; $3 - 1 = 2$; $3 - 2 = 1$. Organize math programs in accordance with known developmental stages of young children. Finally, content should be flexible and able to be adapted to each child's unique abilities and interests.

## Questions Matter: The Quality and the Purpose

Asking meaningful questions means asking a question that has purpose and directs the child to dig deeper into his/her thinking, helping the child build meaningful connections. Creating connections between prior knowledge and current experiences through thoughtful questions also helps create meaningful experiences and facilitates cognitive development.

Asking meaningful questions in the block area (or any other play or activity area):

♦ Watch and listen carefully prior to asking questions.
♦ This observational opportunity provides information on children's intent, goals, and process.
♦ Comments and questions then stem from what is transpiring at the moment.
♦ Be fully present when listening.
♦ Prepare to listen by focusing attention on the speaker.
  ♦ Ask others who would interrupt to wait.
  ♦ Make eye contact.
  ♦ Be mindful of your tone of voice – it should be friendly and inquiring.
  ♦ Be patient while waiting for a response, don't interrupt.
  ♦ Be responsive both verbally and nonverbally.
  ♦ Plan your question keeping in mind the developmental level of your children.
  ♦ Be aware of their prior knowledge.
  ♦ Try using "I wonder…" or "What do you notice …?".
  ♦ Allow plenty of wait time – this is process time.
  ♦ Follow-up questions or make a comment – *"What else can we …?"* or *"Tell me more … ."*
  ♦ Listen carefully to the answer after a question has been asked.

Support each child's investigations and scaffold their understanding through thoughtful questions. See Table 6.1 for examples of meaningful questions for Number Sense development.

**TABLE 6.1** Asking meaningful questions: math: number sense

| Actions | Questions |
|---|---|
| Remember: identify, name, repeat, recall | How many blocks did you use for this house? |
| Understand: describe, discuss, explain, summarize | I notice you used five large blocks for the house. Tell me why. |
| Apply: explain why, dramatize, identify with/relate to | Could you use three more blocks for your house? What might happen? |
| Analyze: recognize change, experiment, infer, compare, contrast | Compare your house to Sarah's building? How are they the same or different? |
| Evaluate: express opinion, judge, defend/criticize | Could you used the same number of blocks of a different size to make a house of the same height? |
| Create: make, construct, design, author | How can you design or create a house using more blocks but making it the same height? |

## Calendar Routines: Alternatives to the Usual

It is usual for school days to begin with a gathering, a circle time where the community of children share, predict, and are introduced to or have reinforced literacy and math skills. A daily activity can typically include the calendar. If we look more closely at this teaching and learning situation, we might realize that calendars can be challenging to understand and predict for young children. They are abstractions which are observed, but not necessarily understood or have relevancy. Temporal time is not yet of importance to young children. Patterns are confusing to identify since each month begins and ends on a different day and not all months are the same length. Here are some alternative ideas for calendar routines.

Alternatives to standard calendar routines can be a paper chain where a new link is added each day changing colors each month or making patterns with the day of the week. This is a plus-one structure of the number system, and is also a visual which can be touched and manipulated. The paper chain calendar creates a timeline which is linear. Use other items to create a linear representation of a calendar such as Unifix®

Cubes. Creating vertical representations of the calendar is also an option. With a column for each month represented with days of the week in different colors or possibly different shapes, line them up next to each other for comparisons as the months pass by. This activity provides opportunity for rich and interesting conversations during community gathering time. Explore and experiment with your own ideas.

## Daily Data

Daily data is information which is of interest and relevance to your young learners organized with numerical values in graphs or grids. The goal of daily data is to introduce ways to organize information in response to a question in a meaningful and understandable manner. This is a simple activity which can be easily integrated into a daily routine either as a stand-alone or as part of your morning gathering.

Your first step is choosing a category or topic for a question and data collection, such as "coats worn to school that day with zippers" or "coats with Velcro" (or "coats with neither" as a category). Choose categories and questions which are simple to begin with and which only two or three variables are being compared until children become more skilled with daily data. Organize your data in charts where the differences and similarities are obvious and understandable. The type of chart you use depends on what you might have on hand, space, or time, or it might be part of a larger lesson on graph organization, representation, and interpretation. Graphs can be symbolic charts, pictographs, or can be made using the actual item (which would work if you are investigating "type of shoe" or some other smallish item).

Interpreting the data is the next important step while determining if the question has been answered. For example, what does a graph or chart based on coat types show, and what do the results indicate for the children? Do more coats have zippers, or Velcro or neither, and what might be the significance of that? How does that information reflect the weather we expect, or our fashion preferences?

The organization and display of data introduce to children ways to manage information in their world and to begin developing the ability to discern similarities (which are easier to find than differences), while also beginning to notice differences among objects. A daily data chart can demonstrate to your students different ways to organize information as well as ways to interpret that information.

Some summary points for these considerations include:

- Choose a topic or category for data collection that has relevance to your students.
- Ask a question about the chosen topic or category.
- Organize your data in charts where comparisons are obvious and understandable.
- Use symbolic charts or pictographs, or the real item if appropriate.
- Topic of choice and the data organization should reflect the developmental abilities and interests of your students.
- Keep the data topic near and relevant for young children – something immediate and apparent.
- Create different charts to represent the same information:
  - Graphs
  - Real or representational
  - Tally
  - Pictures: real images from a camera or cut-outs.
- Determine if the question was answered.

Additional topic suggestions for charts or graphs are:

- Weather
- Outdoor observations
  - Weather changes
  - Animals/plants observed
  - Playgroup activities
- Hair color
- Hair length
- Shoes

- ◆ Clothes
- ◆ Name letters
- ◆ Number of letters in a name (children's names)
- ◆ Favorite food categories
- ◆ Favorite activities
  - ◆ Inside
  - ◆ Outside
  - ◆ With friends
  - ◆ Alone
  - ◆ At school
  - ◆ At home

## Number of the Day

"Number of the day" is a simple and easy way to integrate numeracy into your daily routine. This can be a stand-alone or part of your daily gathering activity. Choose a number appropriate for the developmental abilities and interests of your children. Create a variety of ways to represent that number, such as through a tally, by a picture, in words, through the use of digits, or by equations (if appropriate). Depending on the developmental stage of your students, representation can be symbolic (tally or digit) or the actual item itself. For example, if you are exploring the number five, the digit "5" can be used, or alternatively by five tally marks, five apples, the word "five," or through an equation if appropriate. This activity supports flexibility of thinking about numbers and expressing numbers while developing number sense. Model the behavior, count out loud while touching the objects if using concrete representation. Additional considerations in this area include:

- ◆ Choose a number appropriate for the developmental abilities and interests of your children.
- ◆ Create a variety of ways to represent that number.
- ◆ Representation can be symbolic (tally or digit) or the item itself or something that represents the item such as a picture.
- ◆ Flexibility of thinking about numbers and expressing numbers while developing number sense.

◆ Chart findings so all children are able to visit and revisit this information throughout the day or week.

Another approach to integrating number sense regularly is to choose a number of the week which might connect with other activities being explored, such as a poem or story, or calendar activity.

### Weekly Number

Tie this activity to something learned or discussed recently in class with all the children

♦ a poem or a story
♦ use as a jumping-off point for the weekly number.

## Number Operations

### A Pig Tale
*James Reeves*

Poor Jane Higgins.
She had five piggins,
And one got drowned in the Irish Sea.
Poor Jane Higgins,
She had four piggins,
And one flew over the sycamore tree.
Poor Jane Higgins,
She had three piggins,
And one was taken away for pork.
Poor Jane Higgins,
She had two piggins,
And one was sent to the Bishop of Cork.
Poor Jane Higgins,
She has one piggin,
And that was struck by a shower of hail,
So poor Jane Higgins,
She had no piggins
And that is the end of my little pig tale.

Number operations might seem like a stretch for young children to do or even be introduced to; but if you think of number operations as stories made up of sets where things change by being added to, taken away from, or rearranged, then it becomes intuitive and natural to introduce children to number operations. Using the poem at the beginning of this section, Jane Higgins had a set of five pigs or piggins and through different circumstances she lost them one by one. Her set of five piggins changed over time, and a poem emerged. We can add more to sets or take items away. Multiple sets can be compared, which helps establish the concepts of more than, less than, or equal to. Sets can be broken up or changed by adding additional items. A set can be taken apart so that its broken-up parts are equal to each other or unequal to the other set, and then the parts can be combined to form the whole again. A set of five can be separated into one sub-group of three and one of two, or a sub-group of one and one of four (or five and none).

"A Pig Tale" illustrates principles of number operations for young children to experience. Using a set of five little pig toys, which represents the whole, students follow the poem and remove pigs one at a time from the set at appropriate times, which breaks up the set by separating the original set of five, one by one. From there, children can explore the different attributes of number operations of joining, creating different groups from the whole group and then putting them back together again. While children are exploring sets, you can make notations on chart paper of what happens when a set of five pigs loses one pig, and so on. Number operations help children develop number fluency while building the language of mathematics. Use words expressing quantity, comparisons, greater than, less than, and equal to. Children are ready for these opportunities at early ages and are able to create meaningful learning experiences from their hands-on activities.

# Pattern

### Wind Has Shaken Autumn Down
*Tony Johnston*

Wind has shaken autumn down
Left it sprawling on the ground
Shawling all in gold below
Waiting for the hush of snow.

Children love to experience pleasurable and fun activities and events repeatedly. "Do it again," "Another time," "More" are clarion calls of the young. There is rhythm and pattern to this repetitive behavior which appeals to children and feels satisfactory. Patterns are satisfactory, they are predictable, repetitious, and allow for creativity and abundant play. Activities with young children involving patterns is a natural and joyful opportunity for inquiry and investigation. "Wind Has Shaken Autumn Down" is a poem with lovely and interesting images and patterns: actions (shaken, sprawling, shawling, waiting), seasons (fall, winter), and rhyming sounds (down/ground; below/snow). These few and simple phrases convey a host of opportunities for pattern experiences.

Patterns are a central concept in the study of mathematics. In fact, mathematics is essentially the study of patterns. The Erikson Institute defines patterns as *sequences governed by a rule*, a pattern involves a unit (element which repeats), repetition, and a system of organization. Patterns, however, aren't only studied in the world of mathematics. They can be found in art, language (structure of poetry), science (patterns in DNA), nature (weather patterns), music and song, temporal patterns (seasons, time, months, days of the week, school schedules, home schedules, or any schedule repeated at regular intervals). Even this book is written using a pattern for its structure and organization.

Pattern structures are the ways the different parts in a sequence are organized and related, such as an AB pattern – odd and even; dark and light; loud and soft, fast and slow. When children are able to discern predictable sequences in mathematics, they are better able to make sense of it. In order for children to identify and recognize pattern, they need experience with the concept of repetition and regularity. Patterns are made up of repetition and regularity..

To help your students pattern successfully, they need to be able to recognize and isolate the attributes of objects. An attribute of an object is a characteristic; it describes a property of the object. Take, for example, a solid two-dimensional yellow square; its attributes consist of the color yellow bounded by four sides of equal length with four right angles (the concept of angles can be included if appropriate for your learners). Discerning the relevant characteristics of something in a math-oriented context can take some refinement.

Through careful observation and asking meaningful questions, you will be able to support your students as they begin to recognize attributes of objects and to be more fluid in their thinking with materials for play and exploration which allow this broad way of thinking. Collecting objects that are of interest to your children (keep in mind their own areas of expertise and what is familiar to them) with a range of attributes will help build foundational awareness of attributes and patterning. Some examples of a collection – farm animals or wild animals found locally. Choose objects with an appeal to young children. Using objects with two or more attributes allows for flexibility of sorting and organizing.

The language of patterning gives children the tools needed to communicate ideas and observations about the patterns they see and create. Identify the pattern and describe it; extend the pattern, what comes next?; create, make your own pattern. Extending each of these activities: identify, extend, and create, builds children's skill set, language, and cognitive development. As children become able to identify a pattern, it means they recognize that a pattern exists. Extending the patterns asks the child not only to recognize that a pattern is there, but also to predict the next step. When a child is able to create a pattern of his/her own, ask thoughtful questions about the pattern and have the child explain its sequence.

A pattern needs to repeat itself to be identified as a pattern. Finding patterns in our everyday experiences and in our environment comes naturally to young children and fosters awareness and makes for predictability helping each child to understand and make sense of their world.

## Measurement

This section of our math chapter includes a lot of measurement information. There are seven areas we focus on for young children to explore with you: Quantity and size, order and sequencing, unitization, length, weight, volume, and time. These topics are an important part of building measurement proficiency in young children.

Measurement is a process in which data values (number, units) are given to an attribute of an object or event. Measurable attributes include length, weight, area, volume, time, and temperature. These have been identified as a standard of focus by the National Council for Teachers of Mathematics.

Measurement is a math skill applicable to the real world. It connects to the domains of numbers and geometry which are important skill areas in the realm of mathematics. Geometry has received limited attention in the early years of schooling, but is arguably critical to the development of logic and problem-solving.

Introduce young children to measurement concepts by integrating activities into the daily schedule and making them available at stations around the classroom and outside. The exploration of measurement has practical applications for young children's learning. Measurement activities support learning in other mathematical domains; addressing measurement presents problem-solving opportunities and it encourages active learning, while providing a way to integrate math into other curricular areas.

Foundational skills for measurement begin with young children comparing sizes of objects. This is a regular and everyday event occurring well before formal schooling. Children naturally compare objects, or the quantity of objects, that they have to what they might see in the possession of others. It is important to begin establishing the language of measurement with young children. Awareness and sensitivity to measurement (and size, on an absolute or relative basis) travel along a developmental trajectory. Some concepts of measurement are present at early ages while others bloom later; but all such concepts can be encouraged through ample opportunity for play, interaction, and experience with all the different types of measurement.

## Quantity and Size

Through spending time with young children, teachers are well positioned to be aware of their particular sense of quantity and size and the factors which play into their determination of quantity ("how much") and size ("how big"). Jean Piaget was one of the first to research and explore children's perceptions of quantity and size. Several of Piaget's findings are important when we think about children and the concept of measurement. It should be noted that young children can have difficulty conserving size and quantity. To be able to conserve something means understanding that the concept, thing, or object can stay the same even though other aspects might change. *Conservation of quantity* is when a certain quantity is understood and known on an "operational" basis to remain the same regardless of position, size, or type of container, or arrangement. An example of the "preoperational" stage for this understanding is when a young child is confident that the same amount of liquid held in a short and wide container is "more" when poured into a tall and narrow container. This child who is in the preoperational stage will typically focus on one attribute – such as the height of the container – and deduce that because it is "more" than a smaller container, the volume must also be more.

Another example of this perception involves the *conservation of length* which is when children can perceive an item's length does not change even when moved in comparison to an identical item. Children at a preoperational stage will determine that two items of the same length lined up parallel to each other are the same length; but may change that perception when one item is moved either ahead or behind the other. The child will then conclude that the item ahead is longer – sometimes even though they just observed the two items in direct alignment where they concluded the length was the same.

When working with quantity and size, young children will tend to notice one attribute at a time. Teachers can provide many hands-on experiences comparing quantity and size in order to help young children build understandings while also noticing similarities and differences. Support their investigations with thoughtful and meaningful questions focusing on the differences and similarities of different objects. Over time, children will be able to attend to more than one attribute at once and eventually achieve conservation of quantity (and size).

## Order and Sequencing

This skill requires children to compare objects based on an attribute and build relationships among the objects. To order and create a sequence of a set of objects young children need to be able to isolate specific attributes. There are many toys which provide young children with ordering opportunities. Rings on a peg can go from largest to smallest (or the other way round) when being placed on the peg. Sitting with a child and asking questions about what the child notices supports skill growth in ordering and sequencing. Offer opportunities to introduce children to measurement and comparison terms such as shorter, shortest, taller, tallest, the same, wider than, smaller than, or other comparison words while helping them build an awareness of the relationships which exist among the objects. Ordering situations can then be used, such as asking "does this one goes first?" while also asking the child to explain why, and then introducing the next step (e.g., "then is this one second?") or leaving it open-ended by asking the child which item goes next or second while encouraging a rationale from the child as to why.

## Unitization

Units are additional tools for measuring things. They can be standardized or non-standardized units. Standardized units include inches, feet, miles, ounces, pounds, and gallons, for example, while non-standardized units of measurement can be a paperclip, a pencil, or a finger or any object appropriate to use for non-standardized measurement. When we use a unit to discover the size of an object, we generally break the item down into the individual units of standardized or non-standardized measurement. Measurement using units provides a way to describe that object as it compares to other objects similar to it. For example, using either standard or non-standard units of measurement, two books can be measured using the same unit of measurement (such as inches for standard or paperclips for non-standard) and then compared: this book is 10 paperclips long while the other book is 8 paperclips long: *which book is shorter?* The language and conceptual understanding of measurement and comparisons are developed over time and with a lot of hands-on experiences using both standardized and non-standardized forms of measurement.

Two objects can be easily compared if the unit of measurement is the same. When choosing a unit of measurement, ensure it is appropriate for measuring the chosen object. Research also indicates that when young children measure the same object with multiple arbitrary units, they are more inclined to see the importance of including the unit along with the number when describing their findings. To facilitate this, teachers need to make multiple units of measurement available to their students. For example, if a child is measuring the length of a pencil, they could be given the option to measure it in paperclips or pennies, or with a ruler marked in inches or centimeters.

When comparing measurements, most preschool age children will tend to base their conclusion solely on the number or the unit of measurement. If a child made the following measurements of two pencils of the same length:

Pencil #1 = 3 paperclips
Pencil #2 = 4 pennies

the child may ignore the units of measurement and instead focus on the numbers which would lead him/her to erroneously conclude that pencil #2 is longer than pencil #1 simply because it is 4 units long rather than 3 units long. Many preschool-aged children have not reached the stage at which they can comfortably coordinate both number and unit of measurement and should, therefore, be offered opportunities to participate in activities that draw their attention to the relationship between number and unit of measurement.

In order to identify an appropriate unit of measurement, both the size of the unit and the size of the object must be taken into consideration. For example, it would take a long time (and would increase the chances for error) if the volume of a large bucket was measured by using a teaspoon. Through the use of "either/ or" questioning, teachers can encourage children to thoughtfully consider the interaction between a unit of measurement and the object to be measured.

There are many different activities that can be used in the classroom to make measurement experiences meaningful to children. For example, a child or a group of children have a building project in mind which they want to display on a table. Will the building project fit on the table, and how can they find out? By measuring the table using either standard or non-standard forms of measurement, the child or children can determine what the largest size their building project can be in order to fit on the table.

## Length

One of the easiest measurable attributes for children to perceive is length. Children often come to school with some previous experience and knowledge of length and associated vocabulary. It is not uncommon for adults to observe how a child has grown taller over time. For young children, perceptual comparison of lengths is important. By using objects that are identical except for length, such as pencils or blocks, children are allowed to focus specifically on the concept of length. This way they are able to build a beginning concept of length as an attribute of long, narrow objects. This beginning concept can then be extended by introducing children to unitization activities. Children can use a non-standard unit (same shape blocks) to determine the length of their bodies or a classmate's body length.

See Table 6.2 for examples of meaningful questions teachers can ask students regarding length.

**TABLE 6.2** Asking meaningful questions: measurement: length

| Actions | Questions |
|---|---|
| Remember: identify, name, repeat, recall | How many units (of measurement) tall is your tower? |
| Understand: describe, discuss, explain, summarize | Measure your tower using a different unit. What did you discover? |
| Apply: explain why, dramatize, identify with/ relate to | Did your tower's height change between one unit of measurement and the other? Explain why it did or did not. |
| Analyze: recognize change, experiment, infer, compare, contrast | Use large blocks to build another tower the same height as your first tower. Will you need more units or fewer to measure this different tower? Explain why. |
| Evaluate: express opinion, judge, defend/criticize | Explain why you used more units or fewer units for measuring the length of the new tower. Extension: What would happen to the number of units if you used a different unit, either larger or smaller than the unit you are using? |
| Create: make, construct, design, author | Build a shorter tower with blocks. Use the same unit as the taller block tower was measured by. How much smaller is the shorter tower? |

## Weight

Children can begin to compare weights perceptually by holding two different objects in their hands. They can discuss which feels heavier and which feels lighter. Children often think that bigger objects weigh more and that two objects of the same size weigh the same amount. For this reason, children should be provided with many experiences comparing the heft and feel of different objects. Exploring objects which weigh the same but are different sizes, or objects the same size but of different weights, are some hands-on activities children can engage in to build an understanding of weight. Children can use a balance scale to compare two different objects. After children have had many experiences comparing objects directly, they can be introduced to unitization activities. With the help of a balance scale, children can use a non-standard unit, such as small plastic animals, to determine how many plastic animals different objects weigh. Weight measurement could be included during a study of the local Post Office to provide curricular connections and meaningful opportunities to measure weight, such as boxes and letters. Additionally setting up a farm stand in the play area provides another weight measuring opportunity. Prices of different farm products, measured in chosen units, could be part of the play and learning experience.

## Volume

Volume, which is the amount of space something takes up, is another attribute for children to learn about and begin attending to. Direct comparisons should be used to develop a young child's beginning concept of volume. Perceptual comparisons can be confusing for young children, as mentioned previously, because they may give a disproportional significance to the length (height) attribute of a container. In order to give children direct experiences with volume, a variety of containers with something easy for young children to pour, such as water or sand, is needed. Children can begin to develop an understanding of volume as how much a container holds by filling a container and pouring the contents into another container to compare which holds more. As children gain experience with these direct comparisons, they can be introduced to unitization activities. Presented with bowls of varying size, children can use a non-standard unit (e.g., a scoop) to determine how much water (or sand) is needed to fill the different bowls. Children will likely focus on size – the taller container will often be perceived as holding more water or sand. With ample time and opportunity to explore volume, children will begin to understand the underlying concepts.

## Time

The measurable attributes of time include occurrence and duration. The occurrence of something may be expressed as a point in time (e.g., 11:15 AM), or can occur over a longer timeline (e.g., "in the winter"). Occurrence has a related vocabulary such as hours, days, months, and seasons. Duration involves the time it takes for a specific activity or event to occur. Time of occurrence is a topic which fits well into calendar time. Frame your conversation about time of occurrence with children around events which arrive at special times, such as birthdays, holidays, school days, or days when special events occur. Guide your students in developing awareness of these events and predicting when they might next occur.

Duration relates easily to events which may occur daily and throughout the day for children: how long for an activity, length of time spent reading a story, the amount of time allotted for sharing during circle time, and amount of time for naps or quiet time are just some examples. The duration of an activity occurring throughout the school day presents many opportunities for you to have relevant conversations with your students. Guide children in developing awareness of how long or short a time something takes and have them make predictions or comparisons – does it take longer to read this story than to share my toy with the class?; is outside play time longer than snack time?, these are some ways to talk about length of duration with your learners. Children can focus on familiar elements of different time experiences and may not notice other aspects of time passing until after many opportunities to explore and experience length of duration comparisons. It is through the comparisons that children begin to build up their own system for understanding of time. After children have many opportunities to develop a beginning concept of length of duration, they can begin to participate in unitization activities. For example, during a cooking activity children can use an hourglass to determine how long each child has to stir before their turn is finished.

## Data Analysis

The focus of data collecting and analysis is to answer a question where the answer is not immediately obvious or apparent. Data analysis targets specific skill development, such as counting and classification, while also connecting the process to analysis of numerical and measurable items (Clements & Sarama, 2014). Data collection and analysis serve to lay the foundation for more complex math processes which arise in later years and grades, such as data analysis in science investigations, comparisons between data outcomes, and knowing how to interpret data and the results, which are just some of the more complex applications for data collecting and analysis.

Young children learn the value of data collection when it is stressed in teaching and learning situations. To understand why data collection and analysis are important, children should experience them on a regular basis. Data collection and analysis can be used with most curriculum activities and learning opportunities. Generating a meaningful question where the answer is not obvious is the foundation for this math activity. Make sure the question is relevant and of interest to the children (see also Daily Data on p. 156).

Data must be represented to be interpreted. Data can be represented in many forms. Real items, if appropriate, can be used, such as pictures of the items to be displayed, small toy representations of the object, or symbols like cross marks or tally marks can be used. Data display also has many options – object graphs, pictographs, bar graphs, and tally charts are all ways to display data. Support the development of the language of data analysis through the use of terminology specific to this skill set, such as identifying the different forms of graphs using comparison terms like more than, less than, greater than, and equal to. Asking meaningful questions which require the child to reflect and think about what he/she is seeing are important considerations for developing language and thinking skills.

Once the question has been posed and data collected and displayed, it can then be analyzed by the children with support from the teacher. This underscores the reason for engaging in the process of data collection and analysis. Drawing conclusions from the data is the end result of the activity, and can be supported by scaffolding and the asking of meaningful questions in this process.

## Spatial Relationships

We are always spatially oriented to something or someone in our world. Building the sense of how we can relate to space and objects within that space is the focus of this section, and ultimately will help cognitive awareness of orientation, movement, and spatial thought.

Knowing how to physically move in relation to objects within our physical and visual space requires opportunities to experience our relationship to those objects as well as to how they relate to each other. Spatial relationships and the understanding of them are considered "foundational skills of geometry" (Erikson's Institute Early Math Collaborative, 2014).

Young children regularly seek opportunities to represent their world in play. They recreate familiar spaces and places. The block area and other areas both inside and outside where organization and arrangements of places, spaces, and objects take place are favorite activities for children. Within these activity centers, children can build, organize, and even map the arrangement of the objects and the space in which the objects are placed. Dramatic play is another area where young learners organize objects to represent familiar spaces.

The applicable concepts for these different types of spatial organization and understanding include the idea of space, movement through space, and position in space relative to objects within that space. It is important to note that spatial relationships are not necessarily stable, since animate and inanimate objects may actively move or can be moved. Spatial relationships are not just about the objects and place, they are also about the negative space – the space where no objects are located. Understanding this concept is important for children in order to grasp the "positive" space orientation in relation to the spaces where no items are placed or found. Movement between and among items is enhanced through the language of relationships to items, meaning directional and locational words which build that awareness and competency – words such as right, left, center, over, under, around, next to, between, or on top of are some examples of locational and directional words. Creating maps is also a good exercise in grasping spatial organization.

## Movement

Children may move through space even when stationary. Hands, heads, legs, feet, and fingers can move in many different ways.

Children move in specific ways and with varying abilities. The language of movement helps children understand how they get from one place to another while exploring their own mechanisms for locomotion, whether it is a hand or the entire body. Bodies move through space in relation to other objects; they can move quickly, slowly, smoothly, turning, running, or skipping with different tempos and in other ways. Providing guided and unguided free movement play for young children can help them develop a sense of their own bodies while gaining an appreciation for different experiences of their own movement through space (see the Arts Grid in Table 6.5 at the end of the chapter and Chapter 2 on the Arts for more movement vocabulary and information).

We typically describe events and objects we may experience as they relate to our own position in space. It is important for young children to have many opportunities to experience and describe their own point of view (or perspective) relative to other objects. Understanding a perspective from another's point of view can be challenging, even for adults. This process involves de-centering, which can be learned through experience and the use of spatial orientation language. Maps are a natural extension of spatial awareness. Creating a map takes the child from the concrete experience of objects in space to an abstract representation of the same, translating a three-dimensional experience into a two-dimensional representation.

## Spatial Orientation

This skill set builds foundational knowledge of knowing where you are in relation to other places and spaces (Clements & Sarama, 2014). These abilities develop with experience. Provide the time and opportunity for young children to build these skills through a curriculum which includes spatial orientation experiences and providing space in which children can freely explore movement.

Developing mental maps of different types of space promotes the growth of spatial orientation. Individuals build up knowledge about space and their place in it through experience. There are two categories of knowledge: early-developing and later-developing. The *self-based spatial systems* relate to a child's own position in space and the *external-based reference system* encompasses landmarks in the environment (Clements & Sarama, 2014).

### Spatial Thought

During the second year of life, children develop the ability to think abstractly, to hold symbolic thoughts. Children are able to build mental images of locations. The use of language describing spatial thought and orientation helps build understanding and fluency – some relevant spatial words include on, in, under, up, down; words of proximity include beside, between; and words of reference include in front of, behind (Clements & Sarama, 2014).

Spatial relationships which embrace movement, spatial orientation, and spatial thought are areas not often explored or included in a curriculum for young children. These important skills build the foundation upon which later more complex math skills are based, such as the study of geometry, mapping skills, engineering, and understanding two-dimensional and three-dimensional shapes. Make time and find space for spatial relationship experiences.

## Shapes and Geometry

Mathematics is not a strong focus in many early childhood settings, as was noted in Chapter 1. Geometry and shapes also receive relatively little attention, especially when young children have limited opportunities to explore in-depth two-dimensional and three-dimensional shapes.

Children tend to see "typical" forms of each shape, such as circles, triangles, or squares, but may not recognize less-familiar variations of those shapes. For instance, if a square is turned on its point, it may become a diamond to a child, and it loses its identity as a square in the process.

Identifying shapes by attributes is key to understanding and predicting shape. Shapes can be defined and classified by their attributes. Children may not intuitively recognize that flat faces of solid (three-dimensional) shapes are two-dimensional shapes. Shapes can be combined and separated (composed and decomposed) to make new shapes. Create meaningful learning opportunities for young children to experience in-depth shapes and geometry on an in-depth basis by providing experiences where they compare shapes and identify them. Provide activities where they can compose and decompose two- and three-dimensional shapes. Shapes exist in space with spatial orientations and visualizations – provide time and space for children to explore spatial orientation and visualization. For examples of some shape and geometry activities, see the Shape and Geometry section in Table 6.3.

Use and speak the language of geometry to young children. Help them define attributes of different shapes by identifying the properties of different two- and three-dimensional objects. Focus on the properties of the different shapes, such as number of sides, whether the shape is a closed circle or not, number and type of angles, lines, whether the lines of the shape are parallel, opposite, and whether the shape has right angles. Have children recognize and identify different triangle types, such as obtuse, acute, equilateral, or right, and include different quadrilaterals (four-sided shapes) or other polygons as appropriate for your children and their developmental stage.

Provide a variety of examples of shapes to young children while also providing examples which do not define a shape, such as size or color as well as orientation (Clements & Sarama, 2014). Also let children explore examples which do not define a specific shape, like an open-ended triangle, or one with crossing lines, or curved sides. Hands-on activities promote deeper understandings of shape. Allow ample opportunities for children to physically explore different shapes while interacting with them by asking meaningful and thoughtful questions.

Shapes and geometry are a part of our daily experiences and are all around us, making their inclusion a natural part of the curriculum and easy to integrate into many different activities and learning experiences. Using the language of geometry and shapes while asking meaningful questions guides and supports young children's acquisition and understanding of shapes and geometry. Integrate spatial awareness into children's work on shapes and geometry. Movement opportunities allow children to make shapes while moving through space over time and encourage deeper understandings of shapes in our environment.

## Putting It All Together

Math across the early childhood curriculum is the focus of the concept map in Figure 6.1. This is a spoke-shaped concept map where all concepts radiate out from the central theme: Math Across the Early Childhood Curriculum. Three areas are identified as key aspects for a meaningful early childhood experience in math: Soft Skills are skills children experience in a rich math curriculum which is both broad and deep; Developmental Considerations are skills germane to quality experiences supporting quality learning; and Topics of Early Math. Within each cluster, lines come out from central themes with arrows indicating the directionality of the learning. Eventually all concepts radiate in the direction of the bubble representing math across the curriculum for young children.

See Table 6.3 for math activities for all sections of this chapter.

Additional resources for early childhood teachers are included in the form of two lesson plans.

## Mathematics Lesson Plan #1

### Will It Fit?

This math lesson incorporates a variety of math skills and other domains we have navigated through in this chapter and throughout this book. There are many researchers in the fields of child development, science, and learning who advocate real-life, hands-on experiences that are meaningful and relevant to the young learner. This lesson plan offers a similar opportunity. As with the other lesson plans, this is a template for you to adjust or change as the need or interest dictates. The lesson plan can

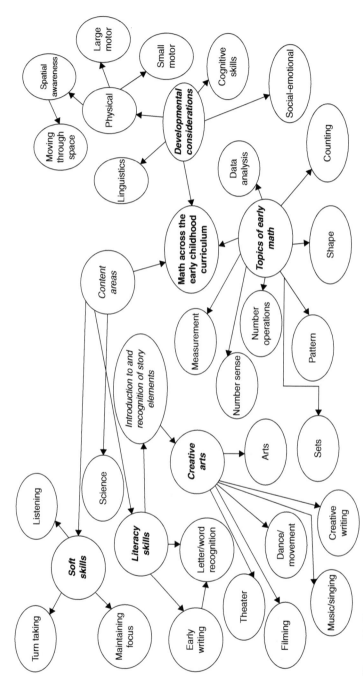

Figure 6.1 Concept map: putting it all together.

**TABLE 6.3** Mathematics activities

| Mathematics | Activities and creative arts |
|---|---|
| Principles of counting | Anything can be counted: when counting with a child, finger-touch each item counted, and ask meaningful questions: "Have we counted those objects?," "How many have we counted?," "Did we count all the objects on the table?" |
| | One-to-one correspondence: use one number per object, event, occurrence, sound, clap, steps, and so on |
| | Speak the same number word in the same order – 1, 2, 3, 4, and so on |
| | Reinforce that the last number spoken in a set represents all the objects in the set |
| | Objects in a set can be counted in any order |
| | Games with counting: hide and seek, fishing for fish, frogs, lizards, count as collect items |
| | Many songs can be made into counting songs to learn the numbers and correlation to objects: "Five Little Monkeys Jumping on the Bed," five little ducks, five current buns, five jellyfish, and so on. You can change the number to suit the needs and skills of your children. |
| | Counting poems can be sung to children as items are counted |
| | Many books have counting themes: *Count to Ten with a Mouse* by Margaret Wise Brown, *1, 2, 3 Fish, Fish, Fish!* by Chad Crouch. Look in the Resources chapter for more book suggestions. |
| Sets | Exploring sets is a natural for most any activity, game, or experience |
| | Make sure the concept of "set" is explained. Game: "What's My Rule?"–"Who Belongs in My Set?" or "Who Does Not Belong in My Set?" |
| | Play games which help children identify attributes and characteristics of different objects |
| | Outline a circle shape on the floor with string large enough to put objects into it and put one object into the circle. Ask children what they notice about the object. Have a variety of additional objects at hand, some with similar attributes and others with no shared attributes. Focus on only one or two attributes at a time. |
| | Set exploration is appropriate for all areas of the classroom and learning stations. Use the vocabulary of sets – same, different, and so on. |

*(Continued)*

**TABLE 6.3** (*Continued*)

| Mathematics | Activities and creative arts |
|---|---|
| Number sense | Share ways numbers are used throughout the day. Keep a chart of all the ways numbers are used. Observe ways children use numbers. |
| | Ask open-ended questions to help children reflect and think about how they use numbers and to help extend their thinking about numbers they use and ways they are used. |
| | Help children identify ways numbers are used throughout the classroom and school setting. Numbers are everywhere and used in a variety of ways not always signifying an amount or a set. Numbers are found on license plates, houses, buildings, zip codes, phone numbers. These numbers indicate a specific type of information not necessarily in mathematical order. |
| | Many books, poems, and songs can convey information about number sense and sets. How many are there? (e.g.,"Three Little Pigs.") |
| | Identify and recognize that the number of a set identifies the quantity of a set and that becomes an attribute of the set |
| | Create matching sets of same numbers which are appropriate to the children's development and skill set |
| | Count items in sets with the children and let them explore ways sets are used in other setting or books. Extension activities can include drawing sets of a specific number. |
| Number operations | Poem: "A Pig Tale" – fun activity for number operations, sets, counting, one-to-one correspondence, and numeracy |
| | The class can create a number story |
| | Each child can illustrate it and either write it up or have help writing it up |
| | Children can then come up with their own stories for number operations. Illustrate them and share |
| Pattern | Poem: "Wind Has Shaken Autumn Down" is a fun poem filled with patterns – words, sounds, seasons, cycles |
| | Keeping in mind the three skills for successful patterning: identify the pattern, extend the pattern, create a new pattern. Patterns can be created, shared, extended, and used in all areas of the curriculum. Patterns are present in all the creative arts: |

| Mathematics | Activities and creative arts |
| --- | --- |
| | In Drama, a pattern of a play can include the introduction, middle, and conclusion; in Singing: patterns include the use of verses and chorus; in Music: phrases are repeated and music pieces have their own predictable pattern; in the Visual arts: patterns include symmetry, using painted patterns, beads or any other item to create a pattern; quilts and quilt making; in Dance: choreographed or free movement phrases can be repeated creating a pattern; in Writing: patterns can include the beginning, middle, ending; in Film/ video: capture visual images of patterns in nature, activities, or any other event which captures the interest of the children |
| Measurement | Measurement covers a lot of ground. It is a comparison skill where lots of hands-on experiences for exploration, testing, experimentation, and learning occur. |
| | Provide many different opportunities for children to explore and test different forms of measurement and with different objects, events, and experiences. We measure lots of things which are not items – footsteps, time, seasons, sounds, experiences, and so on. |
| | Observing, asking open-ended questions on comparisons of objects or events or experiences helps focus the child's thinking. Measurement of an object or event helps to describe the item's qualities more precisely. |
| | Project: children identify a problem in the dramatic play area – they want to add a store to the area. They need to find out if the items they want to add for a store will fit in the space. |
| | Determine items to have for a store |
| | Plan a solution – measure the space and also determine how much space the store and its items will require |
| | Work as a group with the teacher to find a solution, test the solution, revise, and try again |
| Data analysis | Data analysis is part of Daily Data and any data collection and comparison. Data analysis helps children make sense of the information they have collected in response to a data question and collection. It also helps them make sense of their world and the events they observe and experience on a daily basis. |
| | Data charts can be shared and posted for children to revisit and use as examples for other data collections and analysis |
| | Creative arts provide lots of opportunities for data collection in response to a meaningful question |

*(Continued)*

**TABLE 6.3** (*Continued*)

| Mathematics | Activities and creative arts |
|---|---|
| | Art: determining art supplies for a project. Answer a question about what materials to have on hand for an upcoming art project |
| | Children discuss ways to answer the question |
| | Poll the class to see what art materials are preferred for the project |
| | Data chart: list across the top the art material choices. Along the side in a column put the children's names. |
| | Use the actual art material for children to place on the chart next to their name and in the column of art material choice. Determine in advance if the children can choose as many as they want or limit it to a certain number of choices from the list. |
| | Allow children to come up and place their art material choice next to their name in the column of choice |
| | When done polling the class, discuss what the data chart shows |
| | Determine if the question about art materials was answered |
| Spatial relationships | Idea of space, movement through space and time, and position in space relative to objects within that space comprise spatial relationships. How we move, where we move, how we navigate space all require a sense of ourselves and other objects or others within a designated physical space, the boundaries of which are designated by imagination, real objects, or events. |
| Shapes and geometry | Shape activities: find all the circles in a set; feel a shape in a bag, describe it and then name it; explore different shapes and describe their attributes. Combine shapes and separate shapes to create new shapes. Two triangles of the same shape can be combined to make a rectangle (or a rectangle can be separated to make two triangles of the same shape). |
| | Explore shapes which are not regular shapes, such as open circles, triangles with crossing lines |
| | Explore puzzles made of different shapes – find the location where the shape fits |
| | Create new shapes using a variety of different shaped blocks |
| | Ask meaningful questions about different shapes. Describe the attributes of shapes. Does a shape remain that shape when rotated? (If a square is rotated onto its point, is it still a square?) |
| | Explore objects in the classroom for different shapes. |

be expanded with more complex elements for older children, or simplified for those not ready for some of the steps in the lesson.

- ◆ *Age range*: 5/6–8 years of age: kindergarten to early elementary levels.
- ◆ *Instructional objective*: Incorporating math skills in a real-life, hands-on project.
- ◆ *Learning target*: Using the principles of measurement, shapes and geometry, spatial relationships, and numeracy, the children will plan and then construct a puppet theater (taking into account the space required for it), and design and make puppets for a presentation of a favorite story or poem.

To introduce the topic:

- ◆ Activate their prior knowledge about puppet shows. Whole class discussion with chart paper or whiteboard to record and save their ideas. Many children will have experience with puppets but maybe not all. You might have some examples ready to share.
- ◆ Open-ended questions: *"What do you remember?," "What was involved in the puppet show?," "How was it presented?," "What materials were the puppets made of?," "Tell me more,"* and so on.
- ◆ Once you sense the children are ready to move on or have exhausted the list, do a quick review with a bit of adding or re-stating if a contribution was not clear.
- ◆ With the class, choose a short story or poem, making sure the poem has a math theme in it. For illustration purposes here, "A Pig Tale" by James Reeves is used. See the poem on p. 159. "A Pig Tale" involves sets, counting, patterns, and number operations all within a fun and silly poem.
- ◆ Short-term objectives: this can be explored through whole class discussion. Pose your questions and let the children come up with ideas. Record their ideas. The project can be simple or complex as it suits your children's needs,

interests, and skills. This discussion might last for a while so plan to end this part of the lesson/project following the whole class conversation

♦ *"What is needed to present a puppet show?"*
♦ *"How will we go about making a stage and puppets?"*

This discussion will inform the next part of the lesson on creating the stage and puppets. Take good notes while asking open-ended questions about the process of creating both.

## Development

Depending on what your class decided for the stage and the puppets, begin the process of creating both:

- ♦ Assign different children to different tasks which have been identified by you and your students.
- ♦ Size and location of stage – where will it be located? On a table?
  - ♦ Determine materials.
  - ♦ Decide on the size of the stage and then confirm if it fits on the table.
  - ♦ Measure the table. Will it fit? A comparison is being made – comparing the space on the table with the proposed size of the stage.
- ♦ With support from teachers and others, construct the stage.

The stage and the puppets will need to match in size and in the layout. Different types of puppets require specific accommodations.

Hand puppets will need the back of the stage to be opened, puppets on strings will need the top to be opened, silhouettes can have a stick attached to the cutout in the back. Decide on puppet form: hand puppets, silhouettes, string, or cutouts.

What puppets are needed for the play?

- ♦ Five pigs
- ♦ Jane Higgins.

Decide on the size of puppets so they fit just right into the stage setting. Measure the space on the stage where the puppets will be. Too big, too small, or just right? With support from teachers and others, create the puppets.

Now decide on the scenery

◆ Decide on parts of the poem for scenery to be painted or cutouts.
◆ Measure for accuracy in scenery additions.

## Conclusion

◆ Bring all the pieces together for a puppet show to share with others – families and classmates.
◆ Film the process and the outcome to share with those at home and in the community as appropriate.

A lot of work has gone on in each section of the lesson. As noted, it can be simplified or extended depending on your curriculum, daily schedule, student interest and abilities, and space. This project will take up a considerable amount of classroom space while doing it.

◆ Skills: Collaboration, planning, turn taking, direction following.
◆ Math: Counting, measuring, number operations, shape awareness, spatial orientation (moving puppets in a way so they don't crash into each other but move around, near, next to or under each other), spatial thought (imagining where different objects go on the stage), and awareness, geometry (shape of materials for the stage).

Finally, revisit the project process. Ask the children thoughtful and probing questions about the process and outcome of the project and what they learned about putting on a puppet show. Their feedback informs your teaching. What worked?, what could have been different?

♦ Assessment:
  ♦ Were all the children engaged?
  ♦ Were the math objectives achieved or not?
  ♦ Were all the children able to participate?
♦ Developmentally Appropriate Practice:
  ♦ *Families*: Reach out to families prior to the lessons to see if there are any experts or resources. Also let the families know what their child will be doing in class for a few days.
  ♦ *Intentional teaching*: Ask thoughtful, child-centric, open-ended questions, support all learners where they are developmentally.

**A Pig Tale**
*James Reeves*

Poor Jane Higgins.
She had five piggins,
And one got drowned in the Irish Sea.
Poor Jane Higgins,
She had four piggins,
And one flew over the sycamore tree.
Poor Jane Higgins,
She had three piggins,
And one was taken away for pork.
Poor Jane Higgins,
She had two piggins,
And one was sent to the Bishop of Cork.
Poor Jane Higgins,
She has one piggin,
And that was struck by a shower of hail,
So poor Jane Higgins,
She had no piggins
And that is the end of my little pig tale.

# Mathematics Lesson Plan #2

## Spatial Orientation and Mapping

Knowledge of how to navigate in time and space are developed from experience and exploration with spatial orientation and mapping skills. Mental maps of space and where we are in relation to other objects or landmarks encourage development of our sense of spatial orientation and our place in the world.

This is a template for a lesson plan which can be expanded or simplified depending on your needs and the needs and interests of your students.

- *Age range*: 3/4–6/7 years of age: preschool/early elementary.
- *Instructional objective*: Promote development of spatial orientation through hands-on activities.
- *Learning target*: Introduce children to spatial orientation vocabulary while demonstrating each concept in real-time.

To introduce this topic:

- Activate prior knowledge about spatial awareness, orientation, and movement through space.
- Open-ended questions: *"How do we know how to get from one place to another place in our classroom, home, or neighborhood?," "What words can we use to help us explain how we move and get to our destination?"*
- Record words that help describe movement through space and spatial orientation and relationships.
- Use the movement vocabulary:
  - Near
  - Next to
  - Under
  - Over
  - Around
  - Away from
  - Between
  - On top.

Once you sense the children are ready to move on or have exhausted the list, do a quick review with a bit of adding or re-stating if a contribution was not clear.

Read a story about spatial skills development: *Yellow Ball* by Molly Bangs, *Rosie's Walk* by Pat Hutchins, *Follow That Map* by Scot Ritchie, *Piggies in the Pumpkin Patch* by Mary Peterson and Jennifer Rofe., and *Henry's Map* by David Elliot are a few fun examples of books to use with your children. There are many more.

Following your story, let the children explore spatial activities themselves with a simple obstacle course in the classroom and give directions to the children as to how they are to navigate the arrangement:

◆ Start simple, with a few objects for the children to navigate and then add more objects for them to maneuver around.
◆ Let children explore the obstacle course a few at a time and call out the directions while stressing the vocabulary of relevance.
  ◆ *"Go around the chair, stand next to the bookcase, and then step on top of the balance beam."* Create directions suitable to your classroom, your students, and your schedule.

End the lesson whenever you feel the children are done or ready to do something else. Briefly review the lesson with the class before ending.

◆ Assessment:
  ◆ Were all the children engaged?
  ◆ Were all the children able to participate?
  ◆ Were the math objectives of spatial orientation achieved or not?
◆ Developmentally Appropriate Practice:
  ◆ *Families*: Reach out to families prior to the lessons to see if there are any experts or resources. Also let the families know what their child will be doing in class for a few days.

◆ *Intentional teaching*: Ask thoughtful, child-centric, open-ended questions, support all learners where they are developmentally.

## Development

Read another spatial skill development book. Let children try a more complicated obstacle course.

Name the direction or relationship word each time for each child:

◆ Move forward.
◆ Stand next to.
◆ Go around the table.
◆ Step on the balance beam.
◆ Walk close to the chair.

The teacher can keep time and direct movement timing with a drum or other simple percussion instrument. When the drum stops, the child stops and so on.

Have the children experience the obstacle course as many times as they are interested in doing so.

Some children might have difficulty with directionality or proximity language. Hands-on experience with these skills will help build understanding and competency

End the lesson when you sense your children are at a stopping place.

◆ Assessment:
    ◆ Were all the children engaged?
    ◆ Were the math objectives of spatial orientation achieved or not?
    ◆ Were all the children able to participate?
◆ Developmentally Appropriate Practice:
    ◆ *Families*: Reach out to families prior to the lessons to see if there are any experts or resources. Also let the families know what their child will be doing in class for a few days.
    ◆ *Intentional teaching*: Ask thoughtful, child-centric, open-ended questions, support all learners where they are developmentally.

## Extension and Conclusion

Introduce maps to the class, beginning with activating prior knowledge.

- Record their ideas and experiences with maps and then share by reading over the list.
- Read one of the books about maps and how they are used and why they are used. *Follow That Map* by Scot Ritchie, *Henry's Map* by David Elliot are good examples.
- Model mapping of a small part of the classroom which is very familiar to the class with their input and suggestions.

The children will then create a simple map of that same area of the classroom which you have already modeled.

- Assessment:
  - Were all the children engaged?
  - Were the math objectives of spatial orientation achieved or not?
  - Were all the children able to participate?
- Developmentally Appropriate Practice:
  - *Families*: Reach out to families prior to the lessons to see if there are any experts or resources. Also let the families know what their child will be doing in class for a few days.
  - *Intentional teaching*: Ask thoughtful, child-centric, open-ended questions, support all learners where they are developmentally.

Tables 6.4 and 6.5 show the grids of skill sets for Arts and Mathematics. The Arts Grid shows suggested themes/topics: Sets, patterns, collections, measurement, value, games, literature, poetry, movement, shapes, comparisons, integration throughout all content areas, language of math (comparisons, number operations, value, degree, numerical value, number order), set recognition, operations, algebraic thinking, number comparison, identify shapes outside the classroom, data collection and analysis (charts and graphs).

**TABLE 6.4** Mathematics Grid of skill sets and DAP

| Stage | Skill sets | Learning expectations | Scaffolding strategies | Access prior knowledge | Asking good/meaningful/probing questions | DAP (NAEYC, 2020) |
|---|---|---|---|---|---|---|
| Toddler: 13–36 months | Dependence on adults<br>Learning to speak<br>Coordinate sensations and physical activities<br>Think with symbols<br>Imitate and learn from others (Santrock, 2019)<br>Introduction to language of mathematics | Exploration and free play with objects for counting, spatial awareness, shapes, measuring<br>Communicates math ideas verbally and non-verbally<br>Counts to two or three<br>Begins to use number words<br>Begins to solve simple problems<br>Interest in patterns and sequences<br>Matches simple shapes – circle, square, triangle<br>Beginning sorting and classification<br>Beginning time sequence awareness | Verbal encouragement<br>Demonstration<br>Physical support<br>Patience | Observation<br>Asking probing questions<br>Being an attentive listener | *Levels of questioning and expected response or behavior from the child*<br>Remember: identify, name, count, repeat, recall<br>Understand: describe, discuss, explain, summarize<br>Apply: Explain why, dramatize, identify with/relate to<br>Analyze: recognize change, experiment, infer, compare, contrast<br>Evaluate: express opinion, judge, defend/criticize | Relationship with primary caregiver established as warm and welcoming<br>Learn toddler's ways and habits from observation and interactions<br>Acceptance and adjust to toddler's ways and preferences<br>Responsive to toddler's needs<br>Environment appropriate for the toddler with different spaces (quiet, play, small group, individual), with toys to manipulate and explore<br>Indoor and outdoor spaces |

| Preschool: 3–5 years | Curriculum and activities enhances development – physical (small an gross motor), socio-emotional, an cognitive (language: listening, speaking, and understanding) Reading and writing (attendant skills) Introduction to language of mathematics | Continued opportunities for exploration and free play with objects for counting, spatial awareness, shapes, measuring, data collection, and comparisons Begins to use math during daily activities – counting, sorting, matching, comparing Language of math used Rote count to 20 and beyond by ones with increasing accuracy Subitize to determine how many Connect counting to cardinality | Verbal encouragement Demonstration Physical support Patience | Observation Asking probing questions Being an attentive listener Use of a KWL chart or something similar | *Levels of questioning and expected response or behavior from the child* Remember: identify, name, count, repeat, recall Understand: describe, discuss, explain, summarize Apply: Explain why, dramatize, identify with/relate to Analyze: recognize change, experiment, infer, compare, contrast Evaluate: express opinion, judge, defend/criticize | Foster positive relationships Build classroom community Safe, healthy environment promotes independence and exploration w/clear boundaries Spaces promote variety of learning opportunities: small group, large group, individual Different areas arranged to promote different learning styles |
|---|---|---|---|---|---|---|

*(Continued)*

**TABLE 6.4** (Continued)

| Stage | Skill sets | Learning expectations | Scaffolding strategies | Access prior knowledge | Asking good/meaningful/probing questions | DAP (NAEYC, 2020) |
|---|---|---|---|---|---|---|
| | | Demonstrates understanding that the number of objects in a set remain the same regardless of arrangement | | | | |
| | | Begins to write number symbols | | | | |
| | | Recognizes greater than and less than, or equal to up to 10 | | | | |
| | | 1:1 correspondence | | | | |
| | | Addition and subtraction concepts able to demonstrate with fingers | | | | |
| | | Use objects to model addition and subtraction | | | | |
| | | Story problems up to 10 | | | | |
| | | Describes, sorts and classify shapes using attributes | | | | |

(Continued)

Recognizes shapes in environment and is able to name them

Able to identify shapes regardless of orientation

Uses orientation an directionality words (slides, flips, and turns)

Creates simple maps, follows directions during walks

Demonstrates or describe relative position of objects such as up, down, beside, over …

Describes, sorts, and classifies groups of objects suing one or more attribute

Identifies and compares measurable attributes of everyday objects using appropriate language

Use of ordinal language – first, second, third and next and last

**TABLE 6.4** (*Continued*)

| Stage | Skill sets | Learning expectations | Scaffolding strategies | Access prior knowledge | Asking good/ meaningful/probing questions | DAP (NAEYC, 2020) |
|---|---|---|---|---|---|---|
| | | Recognizes patterns and is able to extend, duplicate, create using simple objects<br><br>Concepts of time – yesterday, today, tomorrow<br><br>Use charts and simple graphs to represent data<br><br>Use of non-standard units of measurement to measure objects | | | | Foster positive relationships<br><br>Build classroom community<br><br>Learning environment promotes exploration, initiative, positive peer interaction, and cognitive growth<br><br>Spaces promote variety of learning opportunities: small group, large group, individual |
| Kindergarten: 5–6 years | Curriculum and activities enhances development – physical (small and gross motor), socio-emotional, and cognitive (language: listening, speaking, and understanding) | Continued opportunities for exploration and free play with objects for counting, spatial awareness, shapes, measuring, data collection, and comparisons<br><br>Number and operations integrated into daily activities | Asking questions<br><br>Observation<br><br>Verbal encouragement<br><br>Demonstration<br><br>Physical support<br><br>Patience<br><br>Adult or peer demonstrates skill set | Observation<br><br>Asking probing questions<br><br>Being an attentive listener<br><br>Use of a KWL chart or something similar | *Levels of questioning and expected response or behavior from the child*<br><br>Remember: identify, name, count, repeat, recall<br><br>Understand: describe, discuss, explain, summarize<br><br>Apply: Explain why, dramatize, identify with/relate to | |

| | | | |
|---|---|---|---|
| Reading and writing (attendant skills) | Increased focus on geometry and measurement | Adult or peer engages in activity in parallel play modeling skill and process | Analyze: recognize change, experiment, infer, compare, contrast |
| Develop vocabulary – language of mathematics | Math activities integrated throughout the day throughout the different play activities and spaces | | Evaluate: express opinion, judge, defend / criticize |
| Use appropriately language of mathematics | Reasons abstractly and quantitatively | | |
| | Know number names and the count sequence | | Different areas arranged to promote different learning styles |
| | Count on from a designated number | | |
| | Write numbers from 0–20 | | |
| | Recognize number of objects up to 10 regardless of arrangement | | |

(Continued)

**TABLE 6.4** (*Continued*)

| Stage | Skill sets | Learning expectations | Scaffolding strategies | Access prior knowledge | Asking good/ meaningful/probing questions | DAP (NAEYC, 2020) |
|---|---|---|---|---|---|---|
| | | Compare numbers – greater than, less than, equal to another set | | | | |
| | | Addition is putting numbers together, subtraction is taking apart and taking from | | | | |
| | | Represent addition and subtraction with objects, fingers, mental images, drawings, sounds, acting out, verbal explanation | | | | |
| | | Solve addition and subtraction word problems | | | | |
| | | Identify and describe shapes | | | | |
| | | Describe objects in the environment using name shapes | | | | |

(Continued)

Identify shapes as 2-D or 3-D

Use language to describe relative position of objects in the environment (near, on, below, next to, under, around)

Recognize and describe measurable attributes of objects

Compare two objects with a measurable attribute in common to determine greater than, less than, or equal to

Use terms descriptive of measurement (taller than etc.)

Classify objects

Analyze, compare, create and compose shapes

Model shapes

Compose simple shapes to form larger shapes

**TABLE 6.4** (*Continued*)

| Stage | Skill sets | Learning expectations | Scaffolding strategies | Access prior knowledge | Asking good/ meaningful/probing questions | DAP (NAEYC, 2020) |
|---|---|---|---|---|---|---|
| Primary Grades: 6–8 years | Curriculum and activities enhances development – physical (small and gross motor), socio-emotional, and cognitive (language: listening, speaking, and understanding, word and print knowledge, phonemic awareness)<br><br>Reading and writing (attendant skills)<br><br>Develop vocabulary – language of mathematics | Continued opportunities for exploration and free play with objects for counting, spatial awareness, shapes, measuring, data collection, and comparisons<br><br>Number and operations integrated into daily activities<br><br>Increased focus on geometry and measurement<br><br>Math activities integrated throughout the day throughout the different play activities and spaces<br><br>Reasons abstractly and quantitatively<br><br>Know number names and the count sequence | Asking questions<br><br>Observation<br><br>Verbal encouragement<br><br>Demonstration<br><br>Physical support<br><br>Patience<br><br>Adult or peer demonstrates skill set<br><br>Adult or peer engages in activity in parallel play modeling skill and process | Observation<br><br>Asking probing questions<br><br>Being an attentive listener<br><br>Use of a KWL chart or something similar | *Levels of questioning and expected response or behavior from the child*<br><br>Remember: identify, name, count, repeat, recall<br><br>Understand: describe, discuss, explain, summarize<br><br>Apply: Explain why, dramatize, identify with/relate to<br><br>Analyze: recognize change, experiment, infer, compare, contrast<br><br>Evaluate: express opinion, judge, defend/criticize | Teachers know each child and create a community of learners who support each other<br><br>Children work collaboratively<br><br>Teachers respect children's opinions and ways of thinking<br><br>Classroom environment enhances learning through thoughtful arrangement of furniture and knowledge of each child's learning style<br><br>Learning environment supports exploration, initiative, positive peer interaction and cognitive growth |

(Continued)

Use appropriately language of mathematics

Count on from a designat ed number
Write numbers from 0–30 Recognize number of objects up to 20 regardless of arrangement
Compare numbers – greater than, less than, equal to another set
Addition is putting numbers together, subtraction is taking apart and taking from
Represent addition and subtraction with objects, fingers, mental images, drawings, sounds, acting out, verbal explanation
Solve addition and subtraction word problems
Identify and describe shapes
Describe objects in the environment using name shapes
Identify shapes as 2-D or 3-D

**TABLE 6.4** (*Continued*)

| Stage | Skill sets | Learning expectations | Scaffolding strategies | Access prior knowledge | Asking good/meaningful/probing questions | DAP (NAEYC, 2020) |
|---|---|---|---|---|---|---|
| | | Analyze, compare, create and compose shapes | | | | |
| | | Model shapes | | | | |
| | | Compose simple shapes to form larger shapes | | | | |
| | | Ue language to describe relative position of objects in the environment (near, on, below, next to, under, around) | | | | |
| | | Recognize and describe measurable attributes of objects | | | | |
| | | Compare two objects with a measurable attribute in common to determine greater than, less than, or equal to | | | | |
| | | Use terms descriptive of measurement (taller than etc.) | | | | |
| | | Classify objects | | | | |

**TABLE 6.5** Art Grid of skill sets and DAP

| Stage | Theater/drama/ puppets | Music | Singing | Movement/dance | Visual arts | Creative writing | Photography/Film |
|---|---|---|---|---|---|---|---|
| Toddler: 13–36 months | Simple play – games<br>Finger play<br>Puppet play<br>Poetry/poems | Simple percussion<br>Clapping<br>Patting legs or other body parts or floor<br>Themed music | Nursery rhymes<br>Songs that repeat and build<br>Dynamics of song – high/ low, loud, soft, quick/slow | Simple movement actions<br>Different types of movement<br>Different dynamics<br>Fast, slow | Exploring shapes and lines<br>Exploring marks on paper<br>Exploring color<br>Exploring types of paint application–finger paints, or painting with other items | Placing marks on paper representative or symbolic for concepts, concrete ideas, or objects<br>Simple stories dictated to an adult or simple stories with symbolic marks representative of ideas or objects<br>Poetry/poems | Record either with a camera or video events, objects of meaning, or places<br>Photograph projects for sharing |
| Preschool: 3–5 years | Simple play –games<br>Finger play<br>Puppet play<br>Act out a short story<br>Poetry/poems | Simple percussion<br>Clapping<br>Patting legs or other body parts or floor<br>Themed music | Nursery rhymes<br>Songs that repeat and build<br>Dynamics of song – high/ low, loud, soft, quick/slow | Simple movement actions<br>Different types of movement<br>Different dynamics<br>Fast, slow<br>Move to sound or music | Exploring shapes and lines<br>Exploring marks on paper<br>Exploring color<br>Creating new colors<br>Exploring types of paint application–finger paints, or painting with other items | Placing marks on paper representative or symbolic for concepts, concrete ideas, or objects<br>Simple stories dictated to an adult or simple stories with symbolic marks representative of ideas or objects | Record either with a camera or video events, objects of meaning, or places<br>Photograph projects for sharing<br>Child begins to use camera and video |

(Continued)

**TABLE 6.5** (*Continued*)

| Stage | Theater/drama/puppets | Music | Singing | Movement/dance | Visual arts | Creative writing | Photography/Film |
|---|---|---|---|---|---|---|---|
| Kindergarten: 5–6 years | Simple play – games<br>Finger play<br>Puppet play<br>Act out a short story<br>Take favorite story and devise a play<br>Begin to incorporate the other arts into drama<br>Act out songs<br>Songs with repetition for acting<br>Poetry/poems | Simple percussion<br>Clapping<br>Patting legs or other body parts or floor<br>Themed music<br>Introduce instruments for playing – tambourine, sticks, drums<br>Create simple clapping patterns or rhythms for children to copy and add on to | Nursery rhymes<br>Songs that repeat and build<br>Dynamics of song – high/low, loud, soft, quick/slow<br>Introduce more complex songs with refrains, chorus, and different verses<br>Imitate, extend songs<br>Act out songs<br>Songs with repetition for acting | Circle dance – follow directions (move in, move out, walk slowly holding hands in a circle, and so on)<br>Simple movement actions<br>Different types of movement<br>Different dynamics<br>Fast, slow<br>Move to different sounds or different types of music | Share art of professionals and illustrators<br>Exploring shapes and lines<br>Exploring marks on paper<br>Exploring color<br>Creating new colors<br>Exploring types of paint application– finger paints, or painting with other items<br>Share art of professionals | Continue to develop writing skills and story-making<br>Poetry/poems<br>Placing marks on paper representative or symbolic for concepts, concrete ideas, or objects<br>Simple stories dictated to an adult or simple stories with symbolic marks representative of ideas or objects<br>Continue to develop writing skills and story-making<br>Create stories with a beginning, middle, and end | Record either with a camera or video events, objects of meaning, or places<br>Photograph projects for sharing<br>Child begins to use camera and video<br>Film a play, dance, music performance, an art exhibit |

(Continued)

Find objects in the room or outside to use for percussion or rhythm

Circle dance – follow directions (move in, move out, walk slowly holding hands in a circle, and so on)

Begin to develop more complex movement actions

Fast, slow, high, low, twist, straight, curvy, with a partner, solo, in a group, move in, move out and so on

Teach folk dances or improvise a dance to a well-known and liked song

Art exploration with different mediums, different forms of expression, different materials, different goals

Text with illustrations

Share writings

Poetry – create, share and respond

**TABLE 6.5** (*Continued*)

| Stage | Theater/drama/puppets | Music | Singing | Movement/dance | Visual arts | Creative writing | Photography/Film |
|---|---|---|---|---|---|---|---|
| Primary Grades: 6–8 years | Puppet play<br><br>Act out a short story<br><br>Take a favorite story and devise a play<br><br>Begin to incorporate the other arts into drama<br><br>Act out songs<br><br>Songs with repetition for acting<br><br>Participate in a play<br><br>Choose a theme and write a play centered around the chosen theme | Simple percussion<br><br>Clapping<br><br>Patting legs or other body parts or floor<br><br>Themed music<br><br>Introduce instruments for playing – tambourine, sticks, drums<br><br>Create simple clapping patterns or rhythms for children to copy and add on to<br><br>Find objects in the room or outside to use for percussion or rhythm | Nursery rhymes<br><br>Songs that repeat and build<br><br>Dynamics of song – high/low, loud, soft, quick/slow<br><br>Introduce more complex songs with refrains, chorus, and different verses<br><br>Imitate, extend songs<br><br>Act out songs<br><br>Songs with repetition for acting<br><br>Continue to develop complexity in song format and style | Simple movement actions<br><br>Different types of movement<br><br>Different dynamics<br><br>Fast, slow<br><br>Move to different sounds or different types of music<br><br>Circle dance –follow directions (move in, move out, walk slowly holding hands in a circle, and so on) | Art exploration with different mediums, different forms of expression, different materials, different goals | Create stories with a beginning, middle, and end<br><br>Text with illustrations<br><br>Share writings<br><br>Poetry – read, create, share | Record either with a camera or video events, objects of meaning, or places<br><br>Photograph projects for sharing<br><br>Child begins to use camera and video<br><br>Film a play, dance, music performance, an art exhibit |

| Choose a theme and improvise a story | Layer onto | Layer onto music and dram | Begin to develop more complex movement actions | Continue to explore art from different perspectives, mediums, and themes | Stories reflect themes with complexity of action, characters, and message | Continue to explore ways of using film and video |
|---|---|---|---|---|---|---|
| | | | Fast, slow, high, low, twist, straight, curvy, with a partner, solo, in a group, move in, move out and so on | | | |
| | | | Teach folk dances or improvise a dance to a well-known and liked song | | | |
| | | | Continue to develop complexity in movement and dance | | | |
| | | | Add movement and dance to drama, music, and song | | | |

# 7

# Conclusion

My aim in this book has been to provide classroom teachers with the necessary tools for effective integration of the creative arts with STEM teaching in the early childhood years. Educators need resources, guidance, and models in order to offer all students a rich and high-quality experience with STEM disciplines, and incorporating the arts into existing or future STEM curricula can create and leverage new ways for children to learn those important disciplines. Integrating STEM content with the arts, thus creating STEAM, involves imagination and a willingness to experiment with new approaches while developing an expanded vision. Good teaching is grounded in joy and a belief that our experiences are a journey. This book offers a path for the early childhood educator to pursue during that journey, for the benefit of their young students as well as for the teachers themselves. You as an educator already know a lot about young children and teaching. Imagining, trying, testing, exploring, and learning are the hallmarks of new experiences, whether those experiences are formal or informal or are science-based or art-based. I hope that my readers will take the information shared here as a stepping-off place for them to soar farther on their own, hereby inspiring their students to also soar.

DOI: 10.4324/9781003395614-7

# Resources

## Chapter 1 Introduction

### Websites

Center on the Developing Child at Harvard University. Available at: https://developingchild.harvard.edu/

Erikson Institute Technology in Early Childhood Center. Available at: www.erikson.edu/academics/professional-development/distr ict-infancy-programs/tec-center/

National Association for the Education of Young Children. Available at: www.naeyc. org/

### Bias

Lionni, L. (2015). *Fish is fish*. New York: Andersen Press.

## Chapter 2 The Joy of Creative Arts

### Music and Singing

*Children's songs for guitar* (1976). New York: G. Shirmer.

Kenney, M. (1975). *Circle round the zero*. M M B Music, Incorporated.

McRae, S. W. (1990). *Sing 'round the world: international folksongs for voice and Orff instruments*. Memphis, TN: Memphis Musicraft Publications.Orff-Schulwerk. (1982a). *Music for children*, American Edition, vol. 1 Preschool. London: Schott Music Corp.

Orff-Schulwerk. (1982b). *Music for children*, American Edition. vol. 2. Primary. London: Schott Music Corp.

Pollock Hamm, R. (1987). *Crocodile and other poems. a supplement to music for children*. New York: Schott.

Saliba, K. K. (1982). *Jelly beans and things*. Cock-a-Doodle Tunes.

Samuelson, M. (1978). *Kukuriku: Hebrew songs and dances*. New York: Schott.

*The children's song book* (1983) Shattinger International Music Corporation.

## Art

Sohi, M. E. (2009). *Look what I did with a leaf!* New York: Paw Prints.

Thomas, P. (2007). *Nature's paintbox.* Millbrook Press.

## Dance and Movement

Burnett, M. (1973). *Melody, movement and language.* California: R & E Research Associates.

Haselback, B. (1976). *Improvisation, dance, movement.* St. Louis, MO: Magnamusic-Baton.

Kerlee, P. (1980). *Wake up the earth.* Paul Kerlee.

Kerlee, P. (1983). *Son of wake up the earth.* Paul Kerlee.

Newell H'Doubler, M. (1957). *Dance: a creative art experience by Margaret N. H'Doubler.* Madison, WI: The University of Wisconsin Press.

Weikart, P. (1981). *Movement to the Musica Poetica.* Magnamusic-Baton, St. Louis, MO.

Weikart, P. (1989). *Teaching movement & dance.* High/Scope Press.

Wilmes, L. & Wilmes, D. (1985). *Parachute play.* Building Blocks: Illinois.

## Theater/Drama

Erion, C. & Monssen, L. (1982). *Tales to tell, tales to play: 4 folk tales retold and arranged for music and movement.* London: Schott Music.

Gracie, J. (1986). *The elephant's child.* London: Universal Edition.

# Chapter 3 Science in Early Childhood Education

## Websites

National Association for the Education of Young Children. Available at: www.naeyc.org/

National Science Teaching Association. Available at: www.nsta.org/

Tremblay, R.E., Boivin, M., & Peters, R. De V. (Eds.) (2020). *Encyclopedia of early child development.* Montreal: Centre of Excellence for Early Childhood Development (CEECD) supported by Université Laval and Université de Montréal. Available at: www.child-encyclopedia.com/

## Weather

### *Website*
National Oceanic and Atmospheric Administration. Available at: www.noaa.gov/

### *Literature*
Mckinney, B. S. & Maydak, M. S. (1998). *A drop around the world*. Nevada City, CA: Dawn Publications.

## Nature/Environment
WebsiteNAAEE. Available at: https://naaee.org/

School Garden Resources. Life Lab: School Garden Resources. Available at: https://lifelab.org/for-educators/schoolgardens/

The Nature Conservancy. "Nature Lab." [online] Available at: www.nature.org/en-us/about-us/who-we-are/how-we-work/youth-engagement/nature-lab/school-garden-resources/

Whole Kids Foundation. "School Gardens." [online] Available at: www.wholekidsfoundation.org/school-gardens

## Playscapes
NAAEE. Available at: https://naaee.org/.

Arlitt. "Arlitt Nature PlayScape." Available at: www.arlittchilddevelopmentcenter.com/playscape.

## Nature-Based Early Childhood Education
Children and Nature Network. "Research digest: nature-based learning in the early years." Available at: www.childrenandnature.org/resources/research-digest-nature-based-learning-in-the-early-years/.

Childhood By Nature. "Home. Classic." Available at: www.childhoodbynature.com/.

Childhood By Nature. "Guide to the growing world of nature-based learning." Available at: www.childhoodbynature.com/guide-to-the-growing-world-of-nature-based-learning/.

### *Literature*
Applegate, K. (2021). *Willodeen*. Feiwel Friends.

Aston, D. H. & Long, S. (2013). *A seed is sleepy*. San Francisco, CA: Chronicle Books LLC.

Brown, M., Schenk, B. & Al, E. (1989). *Sing a song of popcorn: every child's book of poems*. London: Hodder & Stoughton.

Depaola. T (2019). *Quiet*. New York: Simon & Schuster.

Dorros, A. (2009). *Feel the wind*. Paw Prints.

Florian, D. (1998). *Beast feast: poems and paintings*. San Diego: Voyager Books.

Frank, J. (1990). *Snow toward evening*. New York: Dial.

Frost, R. & Young, E. (2012). *Birches*. New York: Henry Holt.

Giono, J., Bray, B. & Brockway, H. (2015). *The man who planted trees*. London: Harvill Secker.

Heller, R. (2014). *Chickens aren't the only ones: a book about animals that lay eggs*. New York: Puffin Books.

Kennedy, X. J. & Kennedy, D. M. (1992). *Talking like the rain*. Boston: Little Brown & Company.

Larrick, N. & Raskin, E. (2000). *Piping down the valleys wild: poetry for the young of all ages*. London: Yearling.

Locker, T. & Christiansen, C. (2001). *Seeing science through art: sky tree*. New York: HarperCollins.

Sayre, A. P. (2021). *Thank you, Earth: a love letter to our planet*. New York: Greenwillow Books.

Sidman, J. & Krommes, B. (2018). *Swirl by swirl: spirals in nature*. Boston: Houghton Mifflin Harcourt.

Sohi, M. E. (2009). *Look what I did with a leaf!*: Paw Prints.

Souci, D. S. (1994). *North country night*. London: Yearling.

Thomas, P. (2007). *Nature's paintbox: a seasonal gallery of art and verse*. Millbrook Press.

Tresselt, A. & Sorensen, H. (1992). *The gift of the tree*. New York: Lothrop, Lee & Shepard Books.

Underwood, D. & Derby, C. (2020). *Outside in*. Boston: Houghton Mifflin Harcourt.

Yolen, J. (2005). *Snow, snow*. Astra Publishing House.

## Chemistry

Binczewski, K. & Econopouly, B. (2022). *Bread lab!* Readers to Eaters.

Brown, T. L. (2020). *Perkin's perfect purple: how a boy created color with chemistry*. New York: Hyperion Books.

## Physics
Jorden, T. & Martins, E. (2019). *Physics animated*. Sanger, CA: Familius Llc.

## Rocks

### Website
Geology.com. (2010). *Rocks: pictures of igneous, metamorphic and sedimentary rocks*. Available at: https://geology.com/rocks

NOAA National Centers for Environmental Information (NCEI). Available at: www.ngdc.noaa.gov/

### Literature
Christian, P. & Lember, B. H. (2008). *If you find a rock*. Orlando, FL: Harcourt.

Formento, A. (2014). *These rocks count!* Albert Whitman & Company.

Griffin, M. B. & Bell, J. (2014). *Rhoda's rock hunt*. St. Paul, MN: Minnesota Historical Society Press.

Guillain, C. & Zommer, Y. (2017). *The street beneath my feet*. Lake Forest, CA: Words & Pictures.

Kranz, L. (2021). *There's something about a rock*. Lanham, MD: Rowman & Littlefield.

Miller, P. Z. (2021). *What can you do with a rock?* Sourcebooks, Inc.

Rosinsky, N. M. (2008). *Rocks: hard, soft, smooth, and rough*. Mankato, MN: Picture Window Books.

Salas, L. P. (2022). *A rock can be . . .* Millbrook Press.

## Life Sciences: Water

### Websites
National Marine Educators Association. "Ocean Literacy." Available at: www.marine-ed.org/ocean-literacy/overview

National Oceanic and Atmospheric Administration. Available at: www. noaa. gov/

### Ocean-Based Curriculum
Cerullo, M. M. (2001). *Sea soup*. London: Tilbury House Publishers.

Stevens, B. T. (1999). *Sea soup teacher's guide: discovering the watery world of phytoplankton and zooplankton*. London: Tilbury House Publishers.

### Water-Focused Literature

Baxter, P. (2021). *On grandpa's beach in Maine: a little story about a big rock.* Hidden Oasis Publishing.

Grassby, D. (2011). *A seaside alphabet.* Tundra Books.

Hersey, S. B. (2011). *My Maine.* Little Beach Books.

Ipcar, D. (1977). *Lobsterman.* Camden, ME. Down East Books.

Sayre, A. P. (2021). *Thank you, Earth: a love letter to our planet.* New York: Greenwillow Books.

Smith, G. (2005). *The journey of the little red boat.* George Smith Publishing.

### Natural Resources

Cherry, L. (2013). *A river ran wild: an environmental history.* Columbus, OH: Zaner-Bloser.

## Climate and Weather

### Website

National Oceanic and Atmospheric Administration. "Weather and climate resources." Available at: www.noaa. gov/tools-and-resources/weather-and-climate-resources

### Literature

Beaty, A. (2019). *Sofia valdez, future prez.* New York: Abrams.

Kamkwamba, W. & Mealer, B. (2016). *The boy who harnessed the wind.* Turtleback Books.

Miles, D. & Pinilla, A. (2020). *Climate change: the choice is ours: the facts, our future, and why there's hope!* Cleveland, OH: Bushel & Peck Books.

Reynolds, P. A. & Reynolds, P. H. (2015). *Sydney & Simon: go green!* Watertown, MA: Charlesbridge.

Sayre, A P. (2021). *Thank you, Earth: a love letter to our planet.* New York: Greenwillow Books.

Tariq, A. (2021). *Fatima's great outdoors.* New York: G. P. Putnam

# Chapter 4 The Case for Technology in Early Childhood Education

## Websites

Erikson Institute, Technology in Early Childhood Center. Available at: www.erikson.edu/academics/professional-development/district-infancy-programs/tec-center/

Fred Rogers Institute. Available at: www.fredrogersinstitute.org/

Hatch, The Early Learning Experts. "Interactive Early Learning Solutions Backed by Research." Available at: www.hatchearlylearning.com/

ICDL (International Children's Digital Library). Available at: www.childrenslibrary.org/

Technology and Young Children. (2012). Available at: https://citeseerx.ist.psu.edu/document?repid=rep1&type=pdf&doi=1be1d42ffc83f56f72fdbd205952100922d328b2

## Literature

Cooper, B. & Paprocki, G. (2018). *Little Leonardo's fascinating world of technology*. Layton, UT: Gibbs Smith.

Howard, B. C. (2022). *Polly and the screen time overload*. Tgc Kids.

Smith, K. (2020). *Boxitectt*. Clarion Books.

Snyder, G. & Graegin, S. (2021). *Listen*. New York: Simon & Schuster.

## Technology Texts

Donohue, C. (2015). *Technology and digital media in the early years: tools for teaching and learning*. New York: Routledge.

Howland, J. L., Jonassen, D. H., Marra, R. M., Herrington, J., Parker, J. & Murdoch University (2014). *Meaningful learning with technology*. Frenchs Forest, NSW: Pearson Australia.

# Chapter 5 Young Builders Take on Engineering in Early Childhood Education

## Website

PBS KIDS. "Engineering game." Available at: https://pbskids. org/games/engineering

## Literature

Alling, N. (2014). *When I build with blocks*. Niki Alling.

Howes, K. & Vuković, E. (2019). *Be a maker*. Minneapolis, MN: Carolrhoda.

Sheffield, H. W. (2020). *Brick by brick*. New York: Penguin.

Spires, A. (2017). *The most magnificent thing*. Toronto: Kids Can.

Stevenson, R. L. & Kirk, D. (2005). *Block city*. New York: Simon & Schuster.

Thomson, S. L. & Gonsalves, R. (2003). *Imagine a night*. New York: Simon & Schuster.

Thomson, S. L. & Gonsalves, R. (2005). *Imagine a day*. New York: Atheneum Books.

Van Dusen, C. (2019). *If I built a house*. New York: Puffin Books.

# Chapter 6 A Child's World View Through Mathematics

## Websites

*Encyclopedia on Early Childhood Development*. (n.d.). Home. Available at: www.child-encyclopedia.com/

Erikson Institute. Available at: www.erikson.edu/

NAEYC (National Association for the Education of Young Children). Available at: www.naeyc.org/

## Counting/Numeracy

Atinuke & Brooksbank, A. (2019). *Baby goes to market*. London: Walker Books Ltd.

Barnett, M. & Cornell, K. (2013). *Count the monkeys*. New York: Disney Hyperion.

Brown, M. W. & Richards, K. (2020). *Count to 10 with a mouse*. San Diego, CA: Silver Dolphin Books.

Calmenson, S. (2021). *Dozens of dachshunds*. New York: Bloomsbury Publishing USA.

Cooper, E. (2015). *8: an animal alphabet*. New York: Scholastic Inc.

Crews, D. (2010). *Ten black dots*. New York: HarperCollins.

Crouch, C. (2014). *1, 2, 3 fish, fish, fish!* Piccolo Tableau.

Dee, R. (1990). *Two ways to count to 10*. Basingstoke: Macmillan.

Hoban, T. (1998). *More, fewer, less*. New York; William Morrow.

Hong, L. T. (2017). *Two of everything: a Chinese folktale*. Chicago: Albert Whitman & Company.

Hutchins, P. (1986). *The doorbell rang*. New York: Greenwillow Books.

Kroll, V. L. & O'Neill, P. (2013). *Equal, shmequal*. Watertown, MA: Charlesbridge.

Merriam, E. (2003). *12 ways to get to 11*. New York: Tandem Library.

Mitsumasa, A. (1997). *Anno's counting book*. New York: HarperCollins.

Mora, P. & Lavallee, B. (2000). *Uno, dos, tres: one, two, three*. New York: Clarion.

Murphy, S. J. (1999). *Lemonade for sale*. Sagebrush Education.

Murphy, S. J. & Alley, R. W. (2006). *Animals on board*. Mount Joy, PA: Childcraft Education Corp.

Murphy, S. J. & Petrone, V. (2009). *Double the ducks*. Paw Prints

Murphy, S. J. & Wenzel, D. (2016). *More or less*. New York: HarperCollins.

Ruzzier, S. (2015). *Two mice*. New York: Clarion Books.

Snyder, G. (2020). *Two dogs on a trike*. New York: Abrams.

Soman, D. (2019). *How to two*. New York: Dial Books.

Tang, G. (2017). *Math for all seasons: mind stretching math riddles*. Scholastic Inc.

Verhoeff, N. (2021). *1 smile, 10 toes*. Barefoot Books.

## Shapes and Geometry

Adler, D. A. & Tobin, N. (1998). *Shape up!: fun with triangles and other polygons*. New York: Holiday House.

Allenby, V. (2021). *Shape up, construction trucks!* Toronto: Pajama Press.

Crespo, A. & Medeiros, G. (2020). *Lia & Luís: who has more?* Watertown, MA: Charlesbridge.

Danielson, C. (2019). *Which one doesn't belong?* Watertown, MA: Charlesbridge.

Dodds, D. A. (1999). *The shape of things*, Turtleback Books.

Ehlert, L. (1990). *Color farm and color zoo*. New York: HarperCollins.

Ehlert, L., & Rossner, B. (1989). *Color zoo*. New York: J. B. Lippincott.

Emberley, E. (2006). *Ed Emberley's picture pie*. LB Kids.

Franco, B. (1999). *Grandpa's quilt*. Scholastic Library Publishing.

Hoban, T. (1986). *Shapes, shapes, shapes*. New York: Greenwillow Books.

Hutchins, P. (2015). *Changes, changes*. New York: Simon & Schuster.

Lasky, K. & Hawkes, K. (2005). *The librarian who measured the earth*. Boston: Houghton Mifflin.

Micklethwait, L. (2004). *I spy shapes in art*. New York: Greenwillow Books.

Rosen, M. (1989). *We're going on a bear hunt*. Candlewick Press.

Sidman, J. & Krommes, B. (2013). *Swirl by swirl: spirals in nature*. South Yarra, Victoria: Macmillan Education Australia.

Stevenson, R. L. & Kirk, D. (2005). *Block city*. New York: Simon & Schuster.

Stoll Walsh, E. (2019). *Mouse shapes*. Boston: Houghton Mifflin Harcourt.

Sweeney, J. & Leng, Q. (2018). *Me on the map*. New York: Alfred A. Knopf.

Tompert, A. & Parker, R. A. (1990). *Grandfather Tang's story: a tale told with tangrams*. New York: Alfred A. Knopf.

## Sets and Sorting

Hoban, T. (1987). *Is it red? Is it yellow? Is it blue?: an adventure in color*. New York: Greenwillow Books

Hoban, T. (1998). *Exactly the opposite*. Mulberry Books.

Jenkins, E. & Bogacki, T. (2012). *Five creatures*. New York: Square Fish/Farrar, Straus and Giroux.

Murphy, S. J. & Ehlert, L. (2016). *A pair of socks*. New York: HarperCollins.

Weill, C. (2009). *Opuestos*. Cinco Puntos Press.

## Measurement

Jenkins, S. (2015). *Actual size*. London: Frances Lincoln.

Leedy, L. (2017). *Measuring Penny*. Boston: National Braille Press.

Schwartz, D. M. (2006). *Millions to measure*. Perfection Learning Prebound.

## Spatial Relationships and Map Making

Bang, M. (2022). *Yellow ball*. Purple House Inc.

Elliot, D. & Tuller, T. (2013). *Henry's map*. New York: Philomel Books.

Hutchins, P. (2018). *Rosie's walk*. London: The Bodley Head.

Peterson, M. & Rofé, J. (2010). *Piggies in the pumpkin patch*. Watertown, MA: Charlesbridge.

Ritchie, S. (2009). *Follow that map!: a first look at mapping skills*. Toronto: Kids Can Press.

# References

Brownell, J., Chen, J-Q., & Ginet, L. (2014). *Big ideas of early mathematics: what teachers of young children need to know.* New York: Pearson.

Carr, V. & Luken, E. (2014). Playscapes: a pedagogical paradigm for play and learning. *International Journal of Play, 3*(1), 69–73. DOI: 10.1080/21594937.2013.871965

Center on the Developing Child at Harvard University (2007). http://developingchild.harvard.edu.

Cherry, L. (2013). *A river ran wild: an environmental history.* Columbus, OH: Zaner-Bloser.

Clements, D., & Sarama, J. (2014). *Learning and teaching math: the learning trajectories approach.* New York: Routledge.

Dermon-Sparks, L., & Olsen Edwards, J. (2012). *Anti-bias education for young children and ourselves.* Washington, DC: NAEYC.

DeVries, R., & Sales, C. (2011). *Ramps & pathways: a constructivist approach to physics with young children.* Washington, DC: NAEYC.

Erikson Institute. (2014). *Big ideas of early mathematics.* Harlow: Pearson.

Fred Rogers Center for Early Learning and Children's Media at Saint Vincent College. (2012). *A framework for quality in digital media for young children: considerations for parents, educators, and media creators.* Available at: https://cmhd.northwestern.edu/wp-content/uploads/2015/10/Framework_Statement_2-April_2012-Full_Doc-Exec_Summary-1.pdf

Freeman, S. (2002). *Biological science.* Englewood Cliff, NJ: Prentice Hall.

Gelman, R., & Gallistel, C. R. (1986). *The child's understanding of number* (pp. 73–82). Cambridge, MA: Harvard University Press.

Hirsh-Pasek, K., & Hadini, H. (2020). *A new path to education reform: playful learning promotes 21st-century skills in schools and beyond.* Washington, DC: Brookings Institution.

Jordan, N. C. (2010). Early predictors of mathematics achievement and mathematics learning difficulties. In: Tremblay, R. E., Boivin, M., & Peters, R. De V (Eds.), *Encyclopedia on early childhood development.*

Centre of Excellence for Early Childhood Development (CEECD) supported by Université Laval and Université de Montréal. Available at: www.child-encyclopedia.com/numeracy/according-experts/early-predictors-mathematics-achievement-and-mathematics-learning

Locker, T., & Christiansen, C. (2001). *Seeing science through art: sky tree.* New York: HarperCollins.

Loveless, T. (2021). *Between the state and the schoolhouse: understanding the failure of common core.* Cambridge, MA: Harvard Education Press.

McManis, L. D., & Parks, J. (2011). *Early childhood educational technology evaluation toolkit.* Winston-Salem, NC: Hatch Early Learning.

Merrill, M. L. (2012). *Investigating the nature of third grade students' experiences with concept maps to support learning of science concepts.* UMI Dissertation Services.

Mitsch, W. J., & Gosselink, J. G. (1993). *Wetlands.* New York: Van Nostrand Reinhold.

NAEYC (National Association for the Education of Young Children). (2017). *Big questions for young minds.* Washington, DC: NAEYC.

NAEYC (National Association for the Education of Young Children). (2020). Developmentally Appropriate Practice: A Position Statement of the National Association for the Education of Young Children. Washington, DC: NAEYC. Available at: www.naeyc.org/sites/default/files/globally-shared/downloads/PDFs/resources/positionstatements/dap-statement_0.pdf

NAEYC (National Association for the Education of Young Children). (2022). *Key aspects of early childhood environmental education.* Washington, DC: NAEYC.

NAEYC and Fred Rogers Center. (2012). Key Messages of the NAEYC/Fred Rogers Center Position Statement on Technology and Interactive Media in Early Childhood Programs. Available at: www.naeyc.org/sites/default/files/globally-shared/downloads/PDFs/resources/position-statements/ps_technology.pdf

National Council of Teachers of Mathematics (2002). Six principles for school mathematics. Available at: www.nctm.org/uploadedFiles/Standards_and_Positions/PSSM_ExecutiveSummary.pdf

National Marine Educators Association. (2015). Ocean literacy: the essential principles and fundamental concepts of ocean science.

Available at: http://oceanliteracy.wp2.coexploration.org/ocean-literacy-framework/

NGSS Lead States. (2013). *Next generation science standards: for states, by states*. Washington, DC: The National Academies Press.

North American Association for Environmental Education. (2022). Early Childhood Environmental Education Programs: Guidelines for Excellence. Washington, DC: NAAEE.

NRC (National Research Council). (2007). *Taking science to school: learning and teaching science in grades K–8*. Washington, DC: National Academies Press.

Ogle, D. (1986). A teaching model that develops active reading of expository text. *The Reading Teacher, 39* (6), 564–570.

Santrock, J. W. (Ed.). (2019). *Children*. New York: McGraw-Hill Education.

Strasser, J., & Mufson Bresson, L. (2017). *Big questions for young minds*. Washington, DC: NAEYC.

Vygotsky. L. (1965). *Thought and language*. Cambridge, MA: MIT Press.

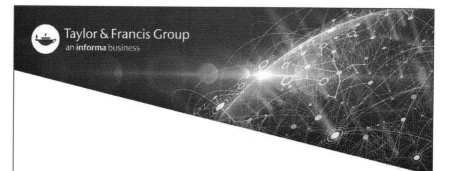